POTENTIAL...

"UNREALIZED ABILITY"

To reach your potential,
just make the changes you need
to grow and improve.

Top 7 REVENUE & PROFIT SOURCES IN YOUR DEALERSHIP

Double Your Net Profit
With Any Of These Simple Solutions

Dealers, Managers & Salespeople
Double Your Net & Personal Income
By Focusing On These 7 Areas

JOE VERDE

The Best Part...

Your Greatest Potential
For More Profit Lies In These
7 Easy To Improve Areas.

BOOKS BY JOE VERDE

• Top 7 Revenue & Profit Sources In Your Dealership

• How To Sell A Car & Close The Sale Today

• Earn Over $100,000 Selling Cars – Every Year

• 38 Hot Tips On Selling More Cars In Today's Market

• 4 Secrets Separate You From Your Competition In Sales!

• 10 Critical Skills Every Automotive Sales Manager Needs

• Manage Your Career In Sales – Goal Setting For Salespeople

• A Dealer's Guide To Recovery And Growth In Today's Market

TOP 7 REVENUE
& PROFIT SOURCES
IN YOUR DEALERSHIP

Joe Verde

Copyright © 2015 by Joe Verde

ISBN#: 978-1-4951-3691-7

2nd Edition Printed in the United States of America

Inquiries should be addressed to Permissions Department, Joe Verde Sales & Management Training, Inc., 27125 Calle Arroyo, San Juan Capistrano, California 92675-2753.

JoeVerde.com – JVTN.com

Toll Free: (800) 445-6217 • International: (949) 489-3780

BAP_08_24_15a

DOES SELLING MORE
EQUAL MORE NET PROFIT?

Maybe – Maybe Not...

So many Dealers and Managers work very hard to sell more units to increase their net profit and are disappointed when the financial statement shows only a small improvement, or no improvement at all.

If that's you, and your goal is to improve your net profit, you may need to trade in some old, ineffective habits that most of us have developed (on where to focus and how to sell) and take a look at these Top 7 Revenue & Profit Sources, so you can sell more units, with higher gross PVR, that translate into higher net profit.

*My goal is to show you
where to focus, and how to...*

DOUBLE YOUR NET PROFIT

*...without spending any extra money
on marketing, advertising or additional staff.*

JOE VERDE

GETS RESULTS FAST

Joe Verde, President of Joe Verde Sales and Management Training, Inc., is the recognized leader in automotive dealer, management and sales training for over 30 years.

Why? Because Joe believes his training should accomplish one goal; get results for each client.

That's why our company and our training is known in the car business as the 'go to source' for immediate sales results and long-term growth. That's also why our company works with over half of the largest dealer groups and Top 500 dealers, and with thousands of other dealerships around the world.

Joe and his team of professional trainers have 60+ years of combined experience teaching Joe Verde sales and management skills and processes. They've spoken to more than 150 dealer 20 groups, ADAs and other industry events, 25 NADA annual conventions, and they hold hundreds of Joe Verde Sales and Sales Management Workshops each year.

Joe's training is exclusive to the automotive industry, and is so effective because it provides *common sense solutions* to every challenge that salespeople, managers and their dealerships face today in selling more vehicles, earning more profit, and retaining their customers for life.

Our sales and management workshops have always been the highest rated classes in the car business, so when Joe pioneered online sales training in 2005 with www.JVTN.com – it was an instant success. As a complete training source, JVTN® gave our dealership customers 24/7 access to all of our courses. And because JVTN® courses mirror our live training workshops, it allows dealers to continue their training after they attend our classes.

From his 'Core 4 Fast Start' for every dealership, to the dozens of continuing education courses online, JVTN® has proven to be the most valuable in-house sales training resource in the automotive industry today.

Why should you take Joe's solutions in this book seriously? Because Joe Verde has successfully 'been there, done that' in every area he teaches, and he will help you get the results you're looking for.

– Kathleen Rittmaster, General Manager
Joe Verde Sales & Management Training, Inc.

TOP 7
REVENUE & PROFIT'
SOURCES IN YOUR DEALERSHIP

You Can Use To

DOUBLE YOUR NET PROFIT
IN JUST 90 DAYS

Table Of Contents

Follow these directions and
you'll increase your income for life.

> **"After your Sales Workshop, I increased my sales from 20 units a month, to averaging 67 per month, and I'm on track to earn $200,000 this year."**
>
> "Joe, the first day of your Sales Workshop, the instructor asked, "What is the one thing you want to get out of this training?" My reply was, "Teach me how to make $200,000 per year!"
>
> At the time, a few of my colleagues laughed and thought it was funny since I was fairly new to the dealership, and because the year had already started.
>
> See, Joe – I've always been a motivated salesperson. After spending 4 years in the Army, 16 months in Iraq and only making $25,000 a year, I fell in love with the car business my first year in sales, when I made $80,000.
>
> By the end of the workshop my attitude was better than ever, my confidence was soaring, and I realized they were all buyers when they were on my lot.
>
> Your 8-Step Sales Process really opened my eyes and truly changed my life. Once I understood how to use the Sold Line Close, it's become my 'go to' close with every customer and it just works!
>
> I was stuck in a 20 car rut for the past 9 years. Two months after your Workshop, I was up to 40 cars per month. Three months after that, I broke the store record at 71 units! My current 90 day average is now 67 units per month.
>
> I asked you to teach me to make $200,000. On my current pace, I am on track to reach my goal. Thanks Joe, for the kick start to awaken me to my full potential!"
>
> *– Abner Elidor, Salesperson, Toyota of North Miami, FL*

There's no question that Abner went above and beyond what 95% of the salespeople will do. But if you do the math on Abner's results, just using an average $2,500 gross per unit, his improvement alone will generate almost $1,000,000 in additional net profit for his dealership. And that's at no additional cost except $1,195 for his training.

Did you realize there is...

$2,905,988
IN NET PROFIT

...potential every year in a 100 unit dealership,
just from the FLOOR TRAFFIC they get now?

Not only is there the realistic potential to turn the typical $500,000 pre-tax net in a 100 unit dealership into $2,905,988 – it can easily be accomplished without spending any more money on Advertising, Lead Generation or by adding a BDC, Social Media Guru, or separate Internet Department.

What about your dealership? Are you willing to be open-minded and work through some easy examples, to see how you can double your own net profit by focusing on 7 areas you can completely control?

The best part...what if doubling your net profit only took you a few months to accomplish, and your benefits would continue for years to come? What if it took you less effort and cost less per month than writing and running a few ineffective ads or trying to buy enough low-profit leads to hit the mother lode?

You don't need more floor traffic to double your net profit!

$2,905,988 is the realistic net profit potential in a 100 unit dealership that is closing 20% of their traffic, and netting $500,000 pre-tax per year. With that much potential, *doubling* $500,000 to $1,000,000 is easy – *with the right focus*.

If you're like most dealerships, you've tried, and are probably still doing almost *everything but* what we'll cover to increase your sales and net profit. Most dealers focus on more **ads**, weekend **events**, more **leads**, **value pricing** every vehicle (really, *lower* your gross to improve profits???), **social media**, adding a **BDC,** and more. *If that's you, have you been growing and improving your net profit?* If not, why not?

Because...

Being 'liked' online, having the cheapest prices in town, or buying more leads and ad space for more floor traffic each month isn't, and never was the problem.

What is there not to understand about the car business today?

- Every customer came to buy and...
- 8 out of 10 people do buy but...
- dealers miss 6 of the 8 buyers on the lot because...
- their salespeople can't sell.

The problem is, and always has been poor selling skills, ineffective processes throughout the sale, and a lack of daily training and daily 'sales management'.

Are You Looking For More Sales And Higher Profits In All The Wrong Places?

While I was waiting to talk to a GM about training one day, I overheard him tell his manager what their sales goal would be for the month.

The first thing his manager asked him was, "So what's the budget?"

If you don't teach your salespeople to 'sell' professionally, spending more on ads and buying more leads won't matter.

I understand why the manager asked that question, because for my first five years selling cars, I was led to believe everything about selling cars had to do with *advertising*, selling *price*, and trying to *split the difference* to make a deal.

For us to *sell more cars,* meant the dealership would be running *bigger* ads and posting *lower* prices on every vehicle. It also meant that our goal was to get any kind of commitment, at any price, so we could put people on paper. That's where we tried to close the sale. How? By dropping the price, of course.

It was confusing. We were told to put everyone on paper *at any price,* but at the same time we were told to pre-qualify everyone on down & payments, trade & payoff, and how soon they planned to buy. Our managers wanted to make sure we were only writing up people who could, and were ready to buy.

Since hardly anybody would agree to buy before we'd even shown them a vehicle, we only gave a few of our prospects a decent demo or presentation, and then we tried to head inside and close them with some form of...

"If the price was low enough, would you buy it now?"

Our managers said they wanted to see every possible deal – but when we brought them a lot of those impossible deals (caused by focusing *just* on price), they'd throw our write ups in the trash. They blamed us for wasting their time, or blamed the customers for not being able to spot a good deal, or blamed the competition for low-balling everybody before we even saw them.

The Top 7 Revenue & Profit Sources

In the past, dealers and managers focused on everything but the very best opportunities to sell more units, at higher gross profits, and they taught almost everyone who worked for them to do the same – by example.

That's why dealers and managers today **still focus on *everything but* the 7 highest revenue sources** and why they're missing 6 out of every 8 sales.

How Important Is The ROI
To You And Your Dealer?

If you want to continually increase profit, measuring your ROI on everything you do isn't just important, *it's a deal breaker*.

At the NADA Convention this year, there were hundreds of vendors who were selling hundreds of ways dealers could improve their sales and revenue. Every product was offered, from car washes and dent repair, to tools in service, lead generation, email solutions, CRMs, DMSs, software in finance, and hundreds of other products.

Let's pretend every product there would generate more sales or more gross for your dealership. Even then, you still have to figure out if it's a *good deal* or a *bad deal* for your dealership. To do that, you have to ask yourself – "What will my real return be on this?"

> *Is this potential return greater than the time and money we'll invest?*

Everything your dealership does to increase sales and profit always requires two things – *time & money*. Logically, your goal is always to make the best choice and get the biggest bang for your time & money.

> *So with every product, you have to ask yourself questions like...*
> *"What type of sale, and what type of gross profit will we get from this?"*

- Will the extra sales generate *good gross* that becomes net profit, or *bad gross* that's eaten up by expenses? (We'll cover good vs. bad gross later.)

- After spending all of your extra time, and after all of your expenses are subtracted, is your final return actually worth the effort?

- Are the extra sales going to be just short-term, one shot deals, or will they also offer long-term benefits that generate continuous revenue?

- After all the smoke has cleared, what will the net effect of the product be on your time, sales volume, gross profit, and net profit?

In our management class, when we talk about the *right & wrong ways* you can generate more gross, it always begs this question...

"Is there really a <u>wrong</u> sale, or <u>wrong</u> gross profit?"

Absolutely. The **worst examples** we'll look at are also the **most common 'wrong ways'** dealers try to improve sales and profits.

While there are dozens of ways you can increase your sales volume, there are only a few ways that actually help you improve your net profit.

*It's those **Top 7 Highest Revenue Sources** we'll focus on.*

Is The Goal In Your Dealership To Have...
❏ Great Months ... or ... ❏ Continuous Growth

Does having a great month, a great quarter, or even a great year mean you're growing? No, it just means you're having a great month, quarter or year.

The recession ended a long time ago, so a couple of months back a dealer told me he didn't want to read my book, "A Dealer's Guide To Recovery & Growth" because they'd recovered from the recession and he didn't need to read it now.

I hear this a lot, because people don't realize the book is 10% on recovery, and 90% on growth; problems, opportunities, strategies, your staff, hiring, job descriptions, managing, etc. Because I talk to hundreds of dealers about growth, I already knew the answer to my question back to him, "Wow, that's great, so you're ahead of your pre-recession unit volume and gross?" His reply...

"Well, no – we're not selling as many units and our gross is lower, but we're making more money now than we were before."

'Recover' means get back to where you were in units, gross and profit, too. I finally talked him into reading the book, and afterwards he told me...

"I wish I had read this years ago, because I can't believe all the things we were doing that cost us sales every month and actually prevented our growth."

Like most dealers, he was making more money from better expense controls, but he wasn't doing what he should to sell more now or to plan for his future growth.

What does 'growth' mean?

'Growth' is simple. It means having record years – year after year. Once you stop having record years, you aren't growing.

Can't you 'buy' growth?

An auto group can buy continuous growth through acquisitions. When the group acquires another dealership, those sales are added to their 'total' sales, so the next year may be a record year, but in this case, not from *improving* what they were doing.

Why can't dealerships buy continuous growth? Because the costs to purchase enough additional traffic to grow will wipe out almost all the potential benefit. Units might go up – but profits won't, or not by much.

When you focus on **The Top 7 Highest Revenue Sources,** you'll sell more units, lower your costs and you'll post record profits, year after year.

Growth can't start until your dealership becomes...
Management Driven ... instead of ... Market Dependent

PICK ONE...

❏ SHORT TERM BUMP

or

❏ HUGE SHORT TERM BUMP

+ LONG TERM GROWTH

Yes – you can get the best of both; an immediate short term gain that also builds long term, continuous growth.

The only catch – you won't get continuous growth year after year, unless you are also willing to take a hard look at how you generate your sales and gross profit.

Let's take a look at that now...

Short Term Sales Increases

Expensive Advertising Generates
Your Lowest & Shortest ROI

Ads usually buy you one result – just one time.
The average ROI on your results from advertising:
$1.^{50} to $2 in return for every $1 spent.

Of course you should advertise *some,* we all need to. It's just very important to remind yourself on almost every ad campaign, that whether you spend money to *buy a sale* through advertising or buy an expensive lead, it usually *only generates just that one $2,500 sale – and usually just that one time.*

There is rarely a second or third sale that comes next month or next year as a result of that liner ad, the lead or the big weekend event – unless you have a sales retention process in place. And focusing on ad-driven prospects brings with it several issues that actually slow or prevent your growth...

4 Consistent Problems With Advertising

1. **Continuously Higher Costs**

   When you analyze the sales that come from your ads, because of the high costs of advertising, an ad-driven sale at $500 costs you ten times more per sale than a sale to a repeat or referral customer. Not only that, but when your business model relies on advertising, you get trapped in a never ending, high-cost spending cycle.

   I know this seems to be true, but it isn't...
   "If we don't advertise we can't hit our numbers."

   Sure, you need big numbers to hit your manufacturer's goals / expectations each month. Missing the goal by even one unit, usually means all the ad money you spent was lost. As you focus instead on these 7 other sources, you'll start hitting your goals without relying on advertising, and that means you'll save money and cut expenses at the same time.

   Just start saying...

   "With daily prospecting and by building our customer base, we can guarantee that we hit our monthly requirements / goals."

2. **Price-Focused / Lower Gross Profit**

   Because most people who respond to the ads and leads you buy are price shoppers – by default, most deals will be price-focused. That, along with poor overall selling skills means lower gross – in both Sales & Finance.

3. Tougher To Close Customers

The closing / delivery ratio for ad-driven traffic is 20% max. It's actually closer to 10%, and if you don't believe that, just hire a spotter to count every opportunity your salespeople have to make a sale. They only log half.

Repeat customers close between 70%-80% of the time. Referrals, and customers from prospecting close 60%-70% of the time. As a group and for the example below, repeat and referrals average 75% closing ratios.

Note: One 'Up' (bird) in the hand is **not** better than
two Repeat or Referral Customers in the (bush) database.

One of the problems with advertising; it generates too much tough to close traffic. Why? Because it takes the focus away from your managers and salespeople developing your business with low cost, high value, easy to close repeat and referral customers who will build your business, year after year.

I had to fight my managers to sell my 30+ every month to my repeat and referral customers, because every time an 'up' walked on the lot it was, "Verde, get off the phone, there's an up on the lot." What he was really saying was, "Verde, stop building our business and go talk to a tough to close price shopper."

To grow, you have to build your business *and* take care of your floor traffic, so you have to balance the two. At first, growth is like a jigsaw puzzle, but once you focus on these solutions, you'll see that all the pieces start to drop into place.

4. Short Term Benefits

80% of the dealerships rely on ad-driven prospects for 70%-80% of their business, so they become trapped into spending huge amounts for ads that produce a very low ROI – just one time.

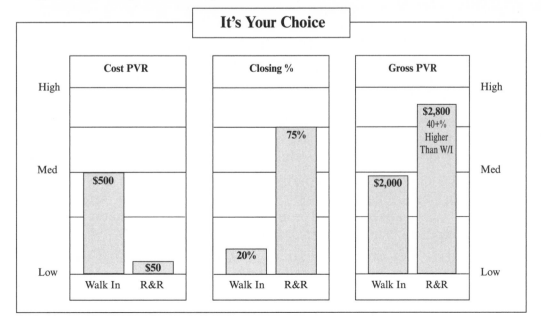

What's Your '<u>Cost Per Unit Sold</u>' From Ads?

*I can tell you now, the **lazy math** almost everyone uses is wrong.*

What do I mean? ... Take our average 100 unit store example that spends $40,000 a month for their online, print, radio and tv advertising...

- Lazy Math ... $40,000 divided by 100 units says the advertising cost per sale is $400 per unit. That's easy, and even though the math may be technically correct – the answer is totally wrong.

- Bad Math ... Why isn't the $400 per unit correct? Because the $400 answer has nothing to do with what it really costs to sell an ad-driven prospect who came from your marketing and advertising sources.

  That 'Bad Math' assumes *all* of the 100 sales came directly from the ads – and we all know that doesn't happen.

  Sure, you want to know the total ad-cost per unit, and that's $400. But that isn't even close to your 'Cost Per Unit Sold From Advertising'.

- More Accurate Math ... Divide the $40,000 by only the sales you know your marketing and ads actually generate.

  That means you stop giving an ad 'credit' just because a vehicle in the ad sold over the weekend, and stop letting managers give their favorite ad sources 'credit' they don't deserve. Only give an ad credit where the credit is due, and you'll find which ads and which sources really work, and you'll save at least 50% on your advertising, too.

- Most Accurate Math ... For the correct / real / scary number, add up every expense for your ad-driven sales – which would include your BDC / Internet / Social Media staff, equipment, rent (plus the costs of your outside marketing & ad sources). Why? Because these departments are only there to generate a sale. That means they're a 'direct cost of sale' just like the ads are.

Business Development – Internet Department

The biggest reason 90% of the dealers **spend tens of thousands of dollars** per month for these additional departments is because they don't have **properly trained** sales managers and salespeople.

They need these additional departments if their salespeople don't know how to prospect, follow up, handle phones and leads, or sell. And that's a result of their managers being promoted, but never educated on how to train, coach and manage their salespeople every day.

*Most dealers spend more on these extra departments **in a single month,** than it would cost them **per year** to train their entire sales and management staff, and **increase sales 25-50% & double or triple their net profit.***

What's <u>Your</u> More Accurate 'Ad Cost'?

Of course, your numbers will be different if you track accurately. Until you do though, use these numbers about the average buyer sources.

- Typical buyer / sales sources...

100	total units sold per month (our typical dealership example)
62%	62 units buy because of the dealership's location & reputation
25%	25 units come from repeat, referral, service, parts
13%	that leaves only 13 possible units generated from advertising

- Using those facts, what's a more accurate cost PVR, just from advertising?

$40,000	advertising cost per month
÷ 13	sales directly from the advertising
$3,077	**cost per vehicle sold from the ads**

"Yeah But - Yeah But - Yeah But
Those aren't right for us – we do much better."

It's OK, if you feel these numbers aren't accurate – just...

- Double your ad returns to **26%** ... that's 26 sales from advertising.
  That drops your cost to just **$1,538 per unit** from advertising.

- Still too high? OK, **pretend 50%** of all 100 deliveries come from ads.
  That drops the cost to just **$800 per unit** from advertising.

- Still too high? **Really highball yourself** and call it **75%** from ads.
  At 75%, it still costs $533 to sell a vehicle from an ad.

And that's still a higher number than anyone ever uses with lazy math.

If You Double Ads ... Will You Double Sales?

After a great presentation from A-2-Z Marketing, you've probably doubled down at least one time on your ad budget hoping to double your sales, or at least hoping to pick up an extra 60 to 70 sales that month.

When the final bell rang at the end of the month though, you only sold an extra 20 to 30 units at best in that 100 unit store, and shook your head in disbelief because you were hoping for so much more. But using the real math on ad sales, even 15 or 20 more sales would double what your ads actually produce.

"Only half of our ads work – we're just not sure which half."

That's true, and if you're tired of wasting 50% of your ad budget, source your ads correctly and you'll find plenty of money for our training to start growing.

Use your numbers in our "Ad Cost Calculator" at JoeVerde.com/calc7

Long Term Growth

Improving People Generates
Your Highest Short & Long Term ROI

Improvements get many results – many times.

Average ROI on improvement from training:

$30 in return per $1 spent.

––––––––––––––

When you improve your processes and a salesperson's selling skills through training, not only will they sell more, they'll also start delivering more of those units to your lowest cost, easiest to close, highest gross repeat, referral, and other existing dealership customers.

Because *improvements* don't require any extra expense, they generate 'good gross' sales and profit. That means the only expense on that sale or that extra gross, is the sales and management compensation on that particular sale, so 60% of the total gross becomes net profit for your dealership.

That's why improving just one salesperson, by just one unit,
becomes a huge profit improvement.

Because the *improvements* from *initial* training are *lasting improvements*, they continue with minimal ongoing training. That means your dealership gets that ROI from training month after month, and year after year.

How To Turn Just One Extra Sale Into
$18,000 In Additional Net Profit Per Year

- Because improvements are long term, one extra sale from improvements and the additional $2,500 in gross from just one salesperson, now becomes 12 more units and $30,000 more in gross profit each *year*.

  $18,000 of the $30,000 extra gross becomes net profit. Why? Because with no new expenses, 60% becomes net profit – from just *one salesperson learning to sell just one more unit* the right way. (See chapter 'Good Gross vs Bad Gross'.)

- To raise your net $180,000 instead ... just improve 10 salespeople by one unit each. Now you have a 10 unit, $25,000 improvement per month – 120 units & $300,000 gross, and an extra $180,000 in net profit in 12 months.

- For a real thrill – fill in your Dealership Potential Calculator at JoeVerde.com/calc7 to *see* the long term value of working with your salespeople to continually improve their performance.

Start Thinking Long Term
That's why we train every day at Joe Verde
and that's why we have record years, every year.

Continuous Growth Is Easy With
Small, Consistent Incremental Gains

Most people ignore minor improvements, but
consistent incremental growth is always more profitable
than a BIG BANG just now and then, will ever be.

- A 6% increase *every month* doubles whatever you're focusing on in a year; sales, gross, F&I, unsold follow up, customer retention, or anything else.

  That means a 100 unit dealership is on their way to doubling sales in a year if they sell 106 next month, and keep improving just 6% every month. That's easy enough just by improving your salespeople a little more each month.

	1 Year											
Month #	1	2	3	4	5	6	7	8	9	10	11	12
Growth	6%	6%	6%	6%	6%	6%	6%	6%	6%	6%	6%	6%
100 Now	106	112	119	126	134	142	151	160	170	180	191	202

- If you want to take the pressure off, go a little slower and improve by 6% per quarter. To improve 6 units per quarter is easy – focus on improvements in skills and processes, and you'll double in 3 years.

  That's not bad – controlling your volume and doubling your sales every 3 years still seems like a pretty good deal, doesn't it?

	Year 1				Year 2				Year 3			
Quarter #	1	2	3	4	5	6	7	8	9	10	11	12
Growth	6%	6%	6%	6%	6%	6%	6%	6%	6%	6%	6%	6%
100 Now	106	112	119	126	134	142	151	160	170	180	191	202

- Wow, seems too quick? That's OK, just change the increase to 3% a month. You'd still be at 142 by the end of the year and that's still awesome.

	1 Year											
Month #	1	2	3	4	5	6	7	8	9	10	11	12
Growth	3%	3%	3%	3%	3%	3%	3%	3%	3%	3%	3%	3%
100 Now	103	106	109	112	115	118	122	126	130	134	138	142

- Can't quite see that? Take it down another notch, to just 3% per quarter, and you'll still be at 142 in just 3 years.

	Year 1				Year 2				Year 3			
Quarter #	1	2	3	4	5	6	7	8	9	10	11	12
Growth	3%	3%	3%	3%	3%	3%	3%	3%	3%	3%	3%	3%
100 Now	103	106	109	112	115	118	122	126	130	134	138	142

*Even if you set a goal to improve 1% for the year and hit it, that's
way better than just holding your breath and hoping for the big one.*

Continuous Incremental Growth Is Easy

Sure, who wouldn't want a hole in one in golf every time, what team wouldn't want to make touchdowns every time they got the ball, and what manager wouldn't want to double sales every month?

So many dealers and managers want to hit that home run every month that they focus on ads, social media, and events instead of focusing on improving something or someone for continuous *incremental* growth, no matter how small it might be.

The secret to our growth for 30 years (27 record years) and to your continuous growth, too, is to make even minor improvements in a salesperson's units or gross regularly.

With discipline – growth is a very simple process...

> 1. Improve by any amount
>
> 2. Stabilize & maintain the improvement
>
> 3. Now repeat 1 & 2

The Top 7 Highest Revenue Sources we'll be covering are the **easiest, fastest, and most profitable areas** you can focus on to improve your sales volume, your gross profit, your net profit, customer retention, and even your customer satisfaction – continually.

*Use your numbers in our calculators at JoeVerde.com/calc7
to see what these small improvements will mean for your dealership.*

Remember ... Dealerships Don't Sell Cars
They Only Provide The Opportunities

One of the most common mis-statements is, "Our dealership sells 100 cars a month." While it's true, by saying it so often, dealers forget the real statement is, "Our salespeople sell 100 cars a month."

Dealerships don't sell cars – they create the opportunities for their salespeople to sell cars. Dealers spend millions each year in operational costs and advertising in their dealerships just to create the opportunities each month for their salespeople to present, demonstrate, close the sale and deliver a vehicle.

Your Salespeople Sell Cars

Dealers spend millions to drive traffic, and then spend pennies to prepare their salespeople for that very expensive, one-shot main chance to make the sale when the customer shows up on the lot.

That same dealer would never have a lube guy try to replace the NAV system, or even do a brake job, because of the risk of messing up a $250 repair and upsetting a customer.

But they'd hire that same lube guy to try to sell a $50,000 car at *$2,500 profit ... to 4 or 5 prospects each day,* but give him no training on how to talk to people, sell a car, close the sale, follow up, prospect or how to work the deal. Then, when the lube guy fails at selling, most managers find a way to blame him for not being smarter or for not trying harder, while *they watch him or her lose a couple of sales and about $5,000 every day* in gross profit.

Too many dealers and managers justify why they miss sales and gross every day, but don't address the core problems. Instead, they double up on ads, marketing and installing new departments to try and make up for not teaching the lube guy, the ex-banker, ball player, waiter, or waitress how to sell cars *so the dealership can improve sales and profit*.

Go figure.

Results

After 30 years in sales, Scott told us...

"I went from 9 to 29 a month from JVTN® and your sales class."

"My manager is a true Joe Verde disciple, and at our store it's the Verde way or no way. Having been in sales as long as I've been, it was a tough transition for me – but boy was it worth it!

I've been in sales for over 30 years, and was averaging about 9 units per month. After training on JVTN® regularly for 6 months and attending your sales class, I truly understood what it takes to be a professional in sales.

Now I understand and believe that EVERYONE is a buyer, I follow your 8 steps to the sale, I go 'to work to work' EVERY DAY, and I give a $50,000 demo and presentation on a $25,000 vehicle and my customers love me!

In just 6 short months, I went from being the 9 car guy to averaging 29 units per month. My best month so far is 34, and my goal is 40 this month.

My manager told me, 'I will make you a believer and I'll make you my top guy,' and thanks to Joe Verde Training, I have made his vision a reality!   Thanks Joe."

– Scott Romero, Salesperson
Finnicum Motor Company, Leesburg, Georgia

✍ **What's the math for Scott's dealership?**

If Scott increased his sales by 20 units per month just by improving his skills and work habits, how many extra units does his dealership sell now?

Scott's dealership sells _____ more per month, and as long as the dealership continues to train Scott to maintain that improvement, his dealership will sell an extra _____ units every year.

In your dealership, how much gross would be generated from an extra 20 units from just one of your salespeople? $ ____, ____ per month and $ ____, ____, ____ per year.

Other than his training, were there any extra expenses needed for Scott's improvement? ❏ Yes ❏ No

Improve your salespeople to improve sales for your dealership.

*Your customers today are actually
'old school' when it comes to value.*

YOUR CUSTOMERS
TODAY

Let's look at the real facts & stats about your customers today and how those facts affect sales, gross, and your personal income.

The potential in these stats for you to improve sales and profit in your dealership is incredible. So grab a notebook, a pen and highlighter and let's get to work.

In each fact about your customers today, you'll want to look for the **potential**, the **problems** and add your input on the **solutions** to turning lost sales and gross into more sales, better gross and improved net profit.

✎ Tip...
Fill in every blank as you go, and turn this
and every section, into a great meeting with all of your managers.

WHICH OF THESE 17 FACTS & STATS ABOUT TODAY'S CUSTOMERS AFFECT YOUR UNIT SALES, GROSS PROFIT ... AND YOUR PAYCHECK?

✍ Circle the # for each fact that affects you and your paycheck and fill in the blanks...

1. **95%+ of prospects have done their research online & know what they want.**

    ✍ How does this fact affect our sales and gross profit potential?_____

    _____

    ✍ How can this affect my personal income?_____

2. **8 out of 10 prospects (78%) who walk on your lot in today's market are buyers, and 90% of them buy within a week.**

    ✍ How does this affect our sales and gross profit potential?_____

    _____

    ✍ The 3 most common reasons we hear for not selling more are...

    _____

    _____

    _____

3. **Prospects today only stop at 2 dealerships before they buy.**

    ✍ How does this fact affect our sales & gross?_____

    _____

    ✍ Do our salespeople & managers realize those 8 buyers (see #2 above) only stop at 2 dealerships before they buy and do we all see the potential to sell more because of this fact?   ❑ Yes ❑ No

    ✍ If not, why?_____

    _____

4. **20% is the average closing ratio (2 of the 10 prospects on the lot).**

    ✍ How does this fact affect our sales and gross profit potential?_____

    _____

    ✍ How much does missing these sales cost me personally each month?
    $ ____, _____ Per Month ... and ... $ _____, _____, _____ Per Year

    ✍ What are we doing that prevents us from delivering more of the buyers on our lot each month?_____

    _____

    _____

5. **71% of customers buy because they like their salesperson.**

✍ How does this fact affect our sales and gross profit potential?_____

_____

✍ List the people in our dealership a customer might talk to, who are not perceived as being very 'likeable'.

_____   _____   _____   _____

_____   _____   _____   _____

6. **71% who didn't buy, said they found a vehicle in inventory they liked, but didn't like the salesperson, management or the process.**

✍ How does this fact affect our sales and gross profit potential?_____

_____

✍ Based on our list above, does this seem realistic at our dealership?__

_____

✍ How much does this cost me personally each month? $_____

7. **86% overall, and 71% of internet shoppers didn't buy what they planned; they bought different colors, equipment, model or brand.**

✍ How does this affect sales, gross and my paycheck?_____

_____

✍ Once they're on the lot, why does offering to locate an exact vehicle ("I can get you one") too early in the process, cost us sales?_____

_____

✍ What are some ways we can sell more from our inventory?_____

_____

_____

_____

8. **80% of their decisions to purchase are made in the demonstration and presentation, on just 20% of the features they care most about.**

✍ How does this affect our sales and gross profit potential?_____

_____

✍ Do 80% of our customers get a demonstration? ❑ Yes ❑ No

✍ If not, why not?_____

✍ Does this cost us sales?_____

✍ How much does this cost me personally each month? $_____

9. **50% do buy on the spot when they get a 'Targeted' Presentation and 'Targeted' Demo on their key 'Hot Buttons'.**

   ✍ What does a 'targeted' presentation and demo really mean, and how does this affect sales, gross and my paycheck? _____

   _____

   ✍ Do all of our salespeople have the skills they need to find our customers' key hot buttons? ❑ Yes ❑ No

   ✍ Which of our salespeople need to improve in this area?

   _____ _____ _____ _____ _____ _____ _____

   ✍ How much would I earn if we all got better at this? $_____

10. **Gross is 40% higher with 'Targeted' Presentations and 'Targeted' Demos that focus on customer 'Hot Buttons', not price.**

    ✍ Why does this make sense?_____

    _____

11. **Price did not make it into the 'Top 10' when JD Powers surveyed buyer concerns about purchasing a vehicle.**

    ✍ If our salespeople focus on price instead of on 'targeted presentations and demonstrations' to build value, is this affecting our sales, our gross, and my paycheck? ❑ Yes ❑ No

    ✍ Why / How? _____

    ✍ How many sales are we losing each month from talking price? ____

    _____

    ✍ How much gross do we lose each month by talking price? $_____

    ✍ How much do those lost sales and gross cost me per month? $_____

    ✍ In what ways do we encourage salespeople to focus on price instead of 'value' during the sale and the negotiation, instead of keeping the focus on the customer's hot buttons and budget (down & payment)?

    _____

    _____

12. **The closing ratio is 5 times higher, and gross profit is 40% higher with repeat, referral and dealership customers compared to walk-ins, phone and internet leads.**

    ✍ Why would this logically be correct?_____

    _____

    ✍ What are we doing, or not doing that prevents us from having more repeat and referral business?_____

    _____

13. **16% of customers pay full price and 30% pay what they're asked to pay. (Too bad more weren't asked to pay full price.)**

   ✍ What percentage of our customers now pay full price? _____%

   ✍ What percentage of our customers pay our full 'asking' price? _____%

   ✍ How much gross would we generate each month if we asked for full price first, instead of asking for just one step above our lowest price? $____

   ✍ What software or other tools have we purchased to help us lower our asking price and gross profit per vehicle? _____
   _____
   _____

   ✍ What else are we doing, or not doing that prevents us from having more full price deliveries and higher gross profit overall? _____
   _____
   _____

   ✍ How much does this cost me personally each month? $_____

14. **8 out of 10 service customers would consider buying from the dealership that services their vehicle.**

   ✍ How does this fact affect our sales and gross profit potential?_____
   _____

   ✍ How many sales do we make each month from service? _____

   ✍ What more could we do every day to capture more of our own customers in service, instead of losing them to the competition?_____
   _____
   _____

   ✍ How much more would I earn each month? $_____

15. **30% of service customers and customers in the dealership's 'sold' database have a family member who'll be buying within 90 days.**

   ✍ How does this fact affect our sales and gross profit potential?_____
   _____

   ✍ We have ___ cust. in service each month ___ x 30% = ____ buyers

   ✍ We have ___ sold cust. in our database ___ x 30% = ____ buyers

   ✍ How many sales do we make now to customers in service and to the people in our customer database each month? _____

   ✍ Based on the # of buyers in service and in our database, how many more sales could we realistically make each month? _____

   ✍ How much more would I earn each month? $_____

16. The average family will purchase about 36 vehicles, lifetime.

✍ What does this really mean for our opportunity to increase sales and gross now, and to build more future sales?_____
_____

✍ What are we doing now to generate more of those 36 sales from our existing customer base?_____
_____
_____

✍ Do we focus as much on building our business internally to our highest closing ratio and highest gross profit customers with effective customer follow up and prospecting by our salespeople, as we spend on trying to generate new leads?   ❏ Yes ❏ No

✍ If not, why not?_____
_____
_____

> *It's 5 times more expensive to generate a new 'hard to close, low gross prospect' than to keep an 'easy to close, 40% higher gross prospect'.*

✍ How many more units could we deliver each month if we train and manage our salespeople to develop our customer base? _____

✍ How much more would I earn each month if we did? $_____

17. 90% of sold customers are never contacted again by their salesperson about purchasing another vehicle.

(Note: 'Perfect 10' letters, BDC contacts, service specials, and automated letters don't count. Why? Because building repeat business relies on continuous contact by the person they like working with.)

✍ What does this really mean for our opportunity to continually improve our sales and profit in the future? _____
_____

✍ How does 90% lack of personal contact by the salesperson affect Customer Satisfaction and Retention? _____
_____

✍ What more can we do to ensure that our salespeople make the personal contacts we need to build our business?_____
_____
_____

✍ If we build our repeat business to 50% of our base now, and maintain our sales to new prospects, we'd deliver ____ more units per month.

✍ How much more would I earn each month if we did? $_____

✍ **Write out your thoughts now.**

What are the most important facts & stats we covered?
Why do those facts stand out to you?

1. _____

   Why? _____

   _____

   _____

2. _____

   Why? _____

   _____

   _____

3. _____

   Why? _____

   _____

   _____

4. _____

   Why? _____

   _____

   _____

5. _____

   Why? _____

   _____

   _____

6. _____

   Why? _____

   _____

   _____

Thinking is the hardest thing for most people to do.

When you remember how to daydream with a purpose, and discipline
yourself to make the time regularly – you can accomplish anything.

Treat This As A 'Working' Book To Help You Improve

1. Before we go deep into your 7 Highest Revenue Sources, take a few minutes and think about the stats we covered in the last few pages. We've already found more than 17 opportunities for you to improve your units, gross and customer retention.

    Even better, each opportunity offers you those extra sales and the extra gross with no extra expense. That means every improvement you make internally generates more 'good gross' for your bottom line.

2. I know your goal is to improve – to do that, just slow down and *think about* how each stat, fact or process we touch on affects your current number of sales and your gross profit.

    Then fill in the blanks in this book on what you're doing or not doing now, or what processes you have or don't have that could cost you sales and gross profit in that particular area. If you will, you'll find it becomes easy to start improving all of the time.

    Remember...
    Mining gold requires digging.

Atlantic Auto Group

"The Joe Verde sales training is the single most important thing we do here.

Our entire sales staff from BDC reps. to General Managers go through this training program a few times a year. In addition, we are all required to complete the Joe Verde online training that is offered.

The results speak for themselves. We have received a 14% increase in new car volume vs. 2013, while at the same time having a nice lift in gross profit.

We consider it the cornerstone to our success. It's one thing we refuse to do without."

– Michael Brown

"Thanks for my best year ever!"

"I have been in the car business for 9 years and training on JVTN® for the past 4 years.

I love JVTN® because it keeps me focused and on track with the basics and believing **all my customers are buyers** – it makes it easier to **build value** by utilizing **more questions** in my presentation, and by knowing that **80%** of sales are made **after the 5th** closing attempt, I'm reminded to always ask for the sale at least 5 times (the right way).

This year, I focused on **building my business** by doing more **sold and unsold follow up**, and implemented the quarterly newsletter in your VSA® (in JVTN®) to my customers.

I sold **211 cars in 2013 and 239 in 2014** for a 13% increase, and by working with more repeat and referral customers my pay soared from $119,000 to $149,000.

Joe thanks to you, I'm not only a sales professional, I am also a great provider for my family with a great career that just keeps getting better!"

– David Wills, Salesperson
Toyota of Danville, Tilton, Illinois

YOUR POTENTIAL

How Many Buyers Are There
And How Much Gross Profit Is Already
On Your Lot Every Month Now?

Our Dealership Example

All of the numbers I use in these examples
are based on a dealership that delivers 100 units,
with an average gross profit of $2,500 per unit.

Save Time – Use Our Online Calculators

To calculate your potential in each solution here
(and in several other areas in your sales department)
use the calculators at JoeVerde.com/calc7

Just enter the correct numbers for your dealership.

WHY DRIVING MORE TRAFFIC IS
NOT A REQUIREMENT FOR MORE PROFIT

Dealerships aren't missing sales from a lack of floor traffic.

Why not?

Do the math below, but use the numbers for *your* dealership and you'll see that there is enough opportunity with the floor traffic you have on your lot right now to double your sales – *and then to double sales again.*

Here's the math on what really happens
in a 100 unit dealership that closes / delivers 20%.

Potential From Floor Traffic Now

**Number of buyers on the lot and
the potential gross profit each month...**

500	People on the lot each month in a 100 unit dealership
400	**Came to buy (8 of 10) and will buy somewhere**
x $2,500	The average gross profit per unit

$1,000,000 **In potential gross profit walks on the lot each month**

And Then...

100	Purchase now for $250,000 in gross profit
300	**Buyers leave without buying (3 out of 4)**
x $2,500	Gross per unit on each *buyer* you don't sell

– $750,000
walks *back off* of the lot each month

How can you get more of that $750,000 each month?
That's what this book is all about.

Find your total potential at JoeVerde.com/calc7

500 PROSPECTS ON THE LOT – 100 DELIVERIES
WHAT HAPPENED TO THE OTHER 400?

(Each silhouette is equal to one prospect on the lot.)

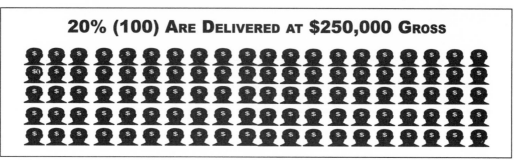

20% (100) ARE DELIVERED AT $250,000 GROSS

300 BUYERS LEAVE
(To buy somewhere else.)

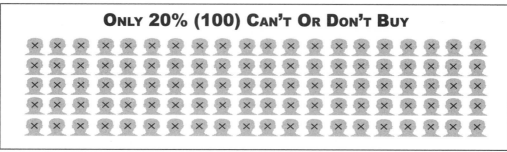

ONLY 20% (100) CAN'T OR DON'T BUY

A lack of floor traffic isn't the problem,
and more floor traffic isn't the solution!

✍ Write Out Your Thoughts On The Opportunity
You See With Your Existing Floor Traffic

_____

_____

_____

_____

_____

_____

_____

_____

_____

_____

_____

_____

_____

_____

_____

_____

_____

_____

_____

_____

_____

_____

_____

_____

Thinking is the hardest thing for most people to do.

When you remember how to daydream with a purpose and discipline
yourself to make the time regularly – you can accomplish anything.

A Floor Traffic Success Story

"My best year ever from JVTN®."

"Joe, this is my 4th year in the car business and I want to thank you for my best year ever in 2014.

I've been training on JVTN® and focusing on **staying off price, slowing down** and **building more value** and of course, I always keep **closing**.

Recently I began focusing on the **transition to finance** and how to plant the seeds for more finance products. What a difference it has made for me, too.

Thanks to your training, I increased my pay in 2014 by 58% taking me to $68,000 this year."

– Neil Levine, Salesperson
Fred Beans Cadillac Buick GMC of Doylestown, PA

> ## "I went from 88 units last year, to almost 200 this year."
>
> "I recently returned from your Sales Workshop and all I can say is WOW, what an eye opener!
>
> In your class, I learned the importance of **slowing down** the sale, being a **better listener** and asking the **right questions** to build **more value** in myself, my product and our dealership.
>
> The results: 2 months ago I sold 13 units, and last month I was the top salesperson, with 21 units and great gross!
>
> Last year, I sold 88 cars and averaged about 7.5 units per month. It's only the middle of June, and I've already sold 77 units for the year. I'm averaging 15.4 units per month now, and that puts me on track for almost 200 units this year.
>
> Joe – thanks for showing me **the path to success** and for providing the tools it takes to get there!"
>
> *– Paul Poltz, Salesperson*
> *Goss Dodge Chrysler Inc., South Burlington, Vermont*

✍ Do the math for Paul's dealership...

If Paul sells 100 more units this year from improving his selling skills, how many extra units did his dealership sell?

Paul's dealership will deliver _____ extra units just from Paul's improvements in his skills and work habits, not from running bigger ads or dropping the price.

In your dealership, how much gross would be generated from an extra 100 units this year?

$ _____, _____, _____

Other than Paul's training, were there any extra expenses?

❑ Yes ❑ No

Improve your salespeople to improve sales for your dealership.

GOOD GROSS
&
BAD GROSS

So much of how and where dealers focus today as they try to increase sales and profit comes from old habits. And when you've done things one way for so long, it's harder to see other options to sell more units.

They've forgotten there are two kinds of gross profit from the sales they make. There's 'good gross', which becomes net profit, and there's 'bad gross' which is eaten up by the expenses it takes to generate the extra sale.

Understanding the difference, and learning how and where to focus on good gross opportunities, turns the monthly grind of trying to make a profit into a step by step process to increase sales, good gross profit, and net profit every year.

WHAT IS GOOD GROSS?

Good Gross comes from what you do *internally* to improve sales or gross, without adding any extra expenses, instead of *externally,* by increasing your expenses with more ads, events, etc. When you don't add any additional expenses to generate another sale ... the only expense to that extra sale and gross is your sales and management compensation of +/- 40%.

60% Of Good Gross Becomes Net Profit

Here are 5 easy examples of where to generate more good gross. Circle which ones you could improve in your dealership with more effective training.

1. *Sell more to the floor traffic you already have now ...* A 100 unit dealership has already paid for the 500 people on the lot and delivers 20% (100). Sell 10 more of those 500, and there's no extra expense. That extra $25,000 gross also becomes **$15,000 in net profit**. Added benefit – lower overall cost per sale.

2. *Get more 'missed' sales back in, with better unsold follow up ...* Put just one more be-back a day on the lot (30 total), deliver 67% = 20 more units for $50,000 gross and **$30,000 in net improvement.** Again, no new expenses, because you already paid to get these customers to show up the first time.

3. *Repeat Customers – Service Customers – Easy Referrals ...* These are all low cost / no cost, easy to sell customers for good gross. Even better, you save $400 in 'cost per sale', and on top of that, these sources generate 40% higher gross profits for even more Good Gross & Net Profit. Sales to these groups **cost you $400 less and generate $800 more per unit in gross,** and are 'Pure Profit' compared to 'walk in' traffic. That's HUGE!

4. *A 100 unit dealership gets 250 +/- incoming sales calls & leads a month...* Improve your 'appointment show' ratio with training (not by adding a BDC) and generate more good gross. Easy improvement: That's 20+ extra units in a 100 unit store, plus **another $50,000 gross and $30,000 net.**

5. *Raise the gross ...* There's no extra expense when salespeople sell value instead of price. Raise the gross $250 on 100 units, and you've picked up $25,000 more, with no new expenses, except your sales and management compensation of about 40%. The rest, **$15,000, is pure profit.**

Good Gross Generates Net Profit & Lowers Your Cost PVR

That's $90,000 in extra net profit (1, 2, 4 & 5) <u>every month</u> in a 100 unit store and another $10,000 in #3 by focusing on repeat and referral business. Plus, all of these examples have already been expensed, so 60% of the extra gross becomes profit.

You are sitting on a Gold Mine, and doubling your net is right around the corner, if you focus on these 'no extra expense' selling opportunities!

Where is your focus now on good gross opportunities?

🖎 *Check the good gross opportunities your dealership focuses on now.*

Then guesstimate how many more units you could sell, and how much more good gross your dealership would earn by improving in each area.

1. Sell more units to the traffic we already have.

Why does selling more of the people already on the lot generate good gross?

_____

Why does this also lower our costs per sale with every extra sale we make?

_____

❑ We can improve, and by improving, I believe we would deliver _____ more units per month for an additional $ _____, _____ in good gross.

Some things we can do to improve are... _____

_____

_____

_____

2. Get more be-backs in, with better unsold follow up.

Why does getting more unsold customers back in generate good gross? _____

_____

Why does this also lower our costs per sale with every extra sale we make?

_____

❑ We can improve, and by improving, I believe we would deliver _____ more units per month for an additional $ _____, _____ in good gross.

Some things we can do to improve are... _____

_____

_____

_____

Henry Ford reminded us that...
"Whether you think you can or can't, you're right."

See how your mind *immediately starts working on solutions* once you switch from thinking about why you can't – to writing out how you can.

Congratulations for taking the time to think through these examples.
Isn't it exciting to realize you actually have control of sales and profits!

---

3. Get more repeat customers, service customers and easy referrals.

Why does getting more repeat and service customers and more referrals generate good gross profit?_____

_____

Why does this also lower our costs per sale with every extra sale we make?

_____

❑ We can improve, and by improving, I believe we would deliver_____ more units per month for an additional $ ___, _____ in good gross.

Some things we can do to improve are... _____

_____
_____
_____

4. Turn more incoming calls and leads into appointments and deliveries.

Why does getting more shows and sales from our phone and internet leads generate good gross profit? _____

_____

Why does this also lower our costs per sale with every extra sale we make?

_____

❑ We can improve, and by improving, I believe we would deliver_____ more units per month for an additional $ ___, _____ in good gross.

Some things we can do to improve are... _____

_____
_____
_____

5. Avoid price, build more value and raise the gross.

Why does improving the gross on every deal by talking price less and building more value generate good gross profit?_____

_____

Why does this also lower our costs per sale with every extra sale we make?

_____

❑ We can improve, and by improving, I believe we would deliver_____ more units per month for an additional $ ___, _____ in good gross.

Some things we can do to improve are... _____

_____
_____
_____

BAD GROSS

Generating more good gross helps you improve your net profit because there are no additional costs.

Generating bad gross does just the opposite, because the expenses to generate the extra sales and gross is eaten up in the extra expenses to make those sales.

WHAT IS BAD GROSS?

Good Gross comes from things you do *internally* to sell more to the opportunities you already have. Bad Gross comes from what you do *externally* to try and help you increase sales or gross, that add even more expenses.

I'm not suggesting you stop any of these activities. Just remember, every example below *can* cost you most or all of the benefit of any extra sales or gross.

1. *Events:* Let's say a 100 unit dealership puts on a big weekend extravaganza.
   Total Investment..........$20,000
   Total Weekend Sales ....32 Units (12 avg. + 20 extra units from the event)
   Extra Weekend Gross ..$50,000 ($2,500 x 20 extra units)
   End of Month Totals...120 units & $300,000 Total Gross

   Awesome! They're up 20 units and $50,000. High-fives everywhere!

	$ 50,000	Total Gross (on the 20 extra units)
–	$ 20,000	Cost of the event
–	$ 20,000	40% Sales & Management Compensation
–	$ 1,000	Or more for bonuses – 'Hat Tricks', etc.
–	$ 2,000	Issues: Trades / rewrites / unwinds, etc.
	$ 7,000	Balance – before any other surprises

   Let's catch our breath from the excitement, and do the real math...

2. *Buying Leads:* A common problem I hear from dealers is, "I can track 10 more sales to leads we purchased, but our volume stayed the same. What happened?" Easy – you just gave hot leads to average salespeople who hit their unit and income comfort zones easier than they would taking ups.

3. *Advertising:* As a new dealership, ads help build your business. But since *everybody* continues to buy the product, after a couple of years, you should have enough sold customers, service customers and referrals to cut your advertising by 80% and still grow every year from repeat and referral business.

A Very True 'LOL' Comment Dealers & Managers Make

"We know only half of our ads work, we're just not sure which half!"

That means a 100 unit dealership wastes $20,000 every month, because they don't know how, or won't track their ad sources accurately.

Manage Your ROI

ROI: Advertising to drive traffic ... $2 in return for every $1 invested.
ROI: Training to sell the traffic you have ... $30 for every $1 invested.

A COMMON EXAMPLE OF BAD GROSS

After my presentation on Phone Rooms & BDCs at the NADA Convention, Robert, a dealer asked me a question I've heard dozens of times...

> *"We sell 100 units, I added a BDC and track 40 units to it each month, but I'm still only selling 100 units – what happened?"*

Like most dealers, Robert installed a phone room because his salespeople focused on price, talked too much, couldn't set appointments, the appointments they set didn't show – and most of the sales they could have made, were lost.

First, why aren't salespeople very good on the phones?

- No Selling Skills ... Phone skills <u>are not</u> a separate skill set, they're just selling skills that a salesperson or manager uses when they pick up a phone.

  For instance, if you can't control a conversation with questions on the lot, if you can't bypass price on the lot, deal with objections or close on the lot, you can't close an appointment on the phone, either.

  80% don't know how to sell, so they can't handle calls correctly either.

- No Management On Handling Phones ... Managers weren't trained on the core selling skills either, and when they were promoted, they weren't taught how to train, coach & manage salespeople daily, much less manage processes like handling incoming calls, prospecting or long term retention.

  Phone leads require selling skills + a clear process + daily management.

OUCH! *Instead of training his salespeople and managers* ... Robert hired another whole team to do their job, hoping that would solve his problem.

- Oops, new problem ... Sales didn't improve because his average and below average salespeople are now getting higher value prospects every day, who close at 40-60% instead of the 10-20% for the walk-ins they'd been relying on. Now they can still sell the same number of units, with even less effort.

Really Bad Gross ... No rocket science needed – hiring two groups of people to do one task because the first group can't or won't, generates extremely bad gross. While there is a correct way to use a BDC effectively, this isn't it.

Good Gross Option ... Your high achievers who average 20-30+ units a month do need help, because they run out of time to do some of the small, but critical tasks on paperwork, deliveries, long term follow up, social media, verifying appointments, etc. that they do, and they need some 'sales assistance' to sell even more units for your dealership.

Note: If you added 1 or 2 sales assistants for your 20-30+ unit salespeople, they'd probably generate more sales and more net per year than a BDC would.

Even Better ... Assistants cost <u>less per year</u> than many BDCs <u>cost per month</u>.

Where do you focus now that is generating 'bad gross'?

✍ List the 'bad gross' areas your dealership focuses on now.

Then guesstimate how many more units you could sell and how much more good gross your dealership would earn by improving in each area.

1. **Right now we...** _____

   _____

   Why does this generate bad gross? _____

   _____

   _____

   Why does this increase our cost per sale? _____

   If we replaced this bad gross process with a more effective good gross process, I believe we would deliver _____ more units per month for an additional $ _____, _____, _____ per month in good gross.

   Some things we can do instead would be to...

   - _____
   - _____
   - _____
   - _____

2. **Right now we...** _____

   _____

   Why does this generate bad gross? _____

   _____

   _____

   Why does this increase our cost per sale? _____

   If we replaced this bad gross process with a more effective good gross process, I believe we would deliver _____ more units per month for an additional $ _____, _____, _____ per month in good gross.

   Some things we can do instead would be to...

   - _____
   - _____
   - _____
   - _____

3. Right now we... _____

_____

Why does this generate bad gross? _____

_____

_____

Why does this increase our cost per sale? _____

If we replaced this bad gross process with a more effective good gross process, I believe we would deliver _____ more units per month for an additional $ _____, _____, _____ per month in good gross.

Some things we can do instead would be to...

- _____
- _____
- _____
- _____

4. Right now we... _____

_____

Why does this generate bad gross? _____

_____

_____

Why does this increase our cost per sale? _____

If we replaced this bad gross process with a more effective good gross process, I believe we would deliver _____ more units per month for an additional $ _____, _____, _____ per month in good gross.

Some things we can do instead would be to...

- _____
- _____
- _____
- _____

Do you have any other bad gross examples?

If you need a spiral notebook to list all of your bad gross processes, that's great and congratulations are in order. Why? Because that means you're sitting on a Gold Mine in sales, gross and profit opportunity that's just waiting for you to start making improvements!

"My units and gross improved 60%!"

"After selling cars for 5 years, I went to Joe's Sales Workshop and realized I had been doing so many things wrong, I was lucky to have the business I did.

After the workshop, I focused on building **value** and following **each step** of the sale. My units and gross per deal quickly improved by 60%.

I've since been promoted to Sales Manager and now I'm training my staff on JVTN® each day. My superiors couldn't be more pleased with our performance. Thanks Joe!"

– Craig Runshe, Sales Manager
Hubbard GM Center, Monticello, Indiana

Your Baseline
Is Your Starting Point
For Improvement

To grow, you have to make improvements. To double your net, the goal is to make those improvements in units and gross, *without* increasing your expenses.

To gauge your profit improvement, you need a clear starting point of reference that we'll call your 'baseline'.

YOUR BASELINE

So that we're all on the same page,
keep these thoughts in mind as you read this book.

1. What's Your Baseline?

It's your starting point for improvements. Because we're talking about growth in unit volume, gross and net profit, you need a starting point, a <u>baseline</u> for profit and expenses, so you can gauge the benefit to your dealership specifically when we cover the 7 different solutions.

> Use your current gross, profit and expenses as your baseline.

All of the additional sales and gross profit improvements we'll cover are 'no expense' improvements, so your baseline expenses don't change.

Your Profit & Expense Baseline
This is your current net profit after all of your business expenses, including advertising.

Because you won't be adding any additional expenses in the 7 solutions we'll cover, the only expense on the extra units you'll sell and the extra gross profit you generate will be your sales and sales management compensation of about 40% of the gross profit you generate.

2. Our Sample Dealership For All Of Our Examples...

To make the math easy to follow, we'll use this sample dealership in all of our solution examples. (Adjust your numbers accordingly.)

Why use a 100 unit dealership as typical? It's easy to scale up or scale down on what we'll cover, depending on your own sales volume, gross and net profit.

Our Sample 100 Unit Dealership
Units Per Month...100
Closing / Delivery Ratio.....................................20%
Average F&B Gross PVR............................. $2,500
Average Sales & Management Comp. 40%
Annual (Pre-Tax) Net Profit..................... $500,000

To do easy math or 'what if'
calculations on these different solutions,
use our online calculators at JoeVerde.com/net7

3. Stats: My Numbers ... vs ... Your Numbers.

If you feel any number I use is too high or low...
No Big Deal – Just Change It.

I always use the commonly known, average industry stats in each area, but no 'average stat' is ever going to be 100% correct for your dealership.

If you feel any number we use in here is too high or too low for your dealership – just use your own dealership's numbers instead. You want to determine *your* potential, so be realistic on any numbers you change, regardless of whether they're higher or lower.

Most tracking in most dealerships is so inaccurate – it would be better to use the common industry stats to begin with, and then start tracking accurately to develop your own baseline for each of the stats we'll cover.

4. Would You Like To Know Your Dealership's Opportunity?

If your goal is to improve your profit...

To quickly see 'how much' profit potential you have, based on what you know about your dealership – use our online calculators.*

There are simple math problems in this book you can just fill in to find your potential and how those improvements affect your income personally.

Or use our online calculators* – so you can do several different 'what if' scenarios – this is one of the features dealers and managers love most.

Take 10 salespeople for instance – each person has a different potential, in different areas of selling. Some could sell 10 more units if they just knew how to sell. Some great closers could sell 5 more just from doing their unsold follow up. Some of your highest achievers may be doing all of their business with repeat customers, and could easily sell 5 or 10 more every month if they just knew the right way to ask those customers for a referral.

You know your people, and the calculators will help you take those differences into account and turn your numbers into what the value is to you and your dealership in taking action to make those improvements.

I guarantee you'll be totally shocked when you calculate what you really see as each person's potential to improve – and even more shocked at how dramatically that improvement affects the bottom line profits for your dealership and your personal income.

Our Online Calculators

Have some 'what if' fun on sales & profit at JoeVerde.com/calc7

> ### *"We're up 50 units and $200,000 per month."*
>
> "We implemented Joe's training and processes about 2 years ago and we have increased our units from 80 per month to 130 per month, and our gross profit is up $200,000 per month.
>
> We are training online with JVTN® on Mon-Wed-Fri, and are targeting specific skills we need. It's just done amazing things for us!"
>
> *– Ben Gonzales, Sales Manager*
> *Pitre Buick GMC, Albuquerque, New Mexico*

✍ Do the math...

Ben's dealership improved by 50 units per month through training, and they'll deliver _____ *more* units every year.

They also increased their gross profit by $200,000 per month, so that's $ ____, ____, ____ *more* in gross profit every year.

Other than his training, does it sound like there were any extra expenses that Ben had? ❏ Yes ❏ No

Those increases are from training their salespeople just 3 days per week, not from advertising or adding new departments.

'A TRICK QUESTION'

What % of improvement
in units and gross do you need to...

DOUBLE YOUR NET PROFIT

✍ *Pick one before you keep reading...*

10% – 15% – 20% – 30% – 45% – 50%
60% – 75% – 80% – 95% – 100%

Remember...
We'll refer to this sample dealership in our examples.
Go to JoeVerde.com/net7 to enter your numbers.

**Sample 100 Unit Dealership
We'll Use For All Examples**

Units Per Month.. 100

Closing / Delivery Ratio.................................20%

Average Gross Per Unit............................. $2,500

Average Sales & Management Comp. 40%

Annual (Pre-Tax) Net Profit....................$500,000

WHAT % OF INCREASE DO YOU NEED IN UNITS & GROSS TO DOUBLE YOUR NET PROFIT?

Have fun and take a 'wild guess' answer to this question:

To double your net profit, what % of increase do you need in units and gross combined, when you focus your improvements on 'Good Gross' options?

✍ *Circle one before you keep reading:*

10% – 15% – 20% – 30% – 45% – 50% – 60% – 75% – 80% – 95% – 100%

Seriously, circle one.

To double your net profit...

If our sample 100 unit dealership focuses on 'Good Gross' sources, when they increase total units sold by just 15 units, from 100 to 115, and when they increase their gross per unit just $375, from $2,500 to $2,875, they'll double their net profit. Yes, that's <u>double net</u> – just from a 15% increase.

How To Double Your Net With Good Gross

Units & Gross Now	100 units at $2,500 per = $250,000 gross per month
Net Profit Now	$500,000 net profit per year
Improve 15%	100 units to 115 & gross from $2,500 to $2,875
	115 units at $2,875 per unit = $330,625 per month
	$80,625 more 'Good Gross' per mo. ($330k-$250k)
	$48,375 in extra net per month at 60% of GG to net
Additional Net	**$580,500 additional <u>net profit</u> per year**
	$500,000 net now + $580,500 extra is...
New Net Profit	**$1,080,500** net per year

116% improvement in net profit just from
a 15% improvement in units and 15% in gross!

Why weren't all of us taught this simple formula?
See the chart on the next page for more examples.

Here's What A 15% Improvement In Net Profit Looks Like, When You Focus On Creating 'Good Gross'

Current Units – Gross – Net Profit	
Monthly Units	100
Gross PVR	$2,500
Total Gross Per Month	$250,000
Total Gross Per Year	$3,000,000
Pre-Tax Net Per Year	$500,000

Double The Net With A 15% Improvement

This is what that 100 unit dealership can do in net profits by focusing their improvements on the opportunities we'll cover that do not increase their expenses.

Have fun with your own 'what ifs' using our calculators.
JoeVerde.com/calc7

New Results From Improvements		% Unit & Gross Improvement					
		5.0%	10.0%	15.0%	20.0%	25.0%	50.0%
Monthly Units Now	100	105	110	115	120	125	150
Gross PVR Now	$2,500	$ 2,625	$ 2,750	$ 2,875	$ 3,000	$ 3,125	$ 3,750
Gross Profit Per Month		$ 275,625	$ 302,500	$ 330,625	$ 360,000	$ 390,625	$ 562,500
Gross Profit Per Year		$ 3,307,500	$ 3,630,000	$ 3,967,500	$ 4,320,000	$ 4,687,500	$ 6,750,000
Additional New 'Good' Gross Per Month		$ 25,625	$ 52,500	$ 80,625	$ 110,000	$ 140,625	$ 312,500
Additional Net Profit / Mo. From 'Good' Gross		$ 15,375	$ 31,500	$ 48,375	$ 66,000	$ 84,375	$ 187,500
Additional Net Profit / Year From 'Good' Gross		$ 184,500	$ 378,000	$ 580,500	$ 792,000	$ 1,012,500	$ 2,250,000
Current Net Per Year		$ 500,000	$ 500,000	$ 500,000	$ 500,000	$ 500,000	$ 500,000
New Pre-Tax Net Per Year		$ 684,500	$ 878,000	$ 1,080,500	$ 1,292,000	$ 1,512,500	$ 2,750,000
% Improvement In Net Profit		37%	76%	116%	158%	203%	450%

Do your own 'what if' calculations for your dealership.
Just use our calculator at JoeVerde.com/net7

Using Your Numbers...
Do The Math On Doubling Your Net Profit

For a quick example on Good Gross, use our online calculator* or just fill in these blanks on what it takes for your dealership to double your net profit.

Use a 15% improvement in units, a 15% improvement in gross, and 60% to net profit your first time through. Then change any of those numbers if you don't feel the 15% improvement, or the 60% to net is possible for your dealership.

1. **Total 'Retail' Gross Per Month Now**

    a. $ ____, ____, ____

2. **Pre-Tax Annual Net Profit Now**

    a. $ ____, ____, ____ per month

    b. $ ____, ____, ____ per year

3. **90 Day Unit Avg**   _____ **per month**

    a.   x   15%   improvement

    b.   =   _____ new avg total units

4. **90 Day Gross PVR** $ ____, ____ **now**

    a.   x   15%   good gross improvement

    b.   =   _____ new avg gross PVR

5. **New Total Gross Per Month**

    a.   3b   _____ total new units

    b.   x   4b $ _____ total new gross PVR

    c.   = $ ____, ____, ____ new gross per mo.

    d.   –   1a $ ____, ____, ____ current gross now

    e.   = $ ____, ____, ____ additional good gross

    f.   x   60%   of good gross (e) becomes net profit

    g.   = $ ____, ____, ____ additional net profit

6. **New Pre-Tax Net Profit Per Year**

    a.   5g $ ____, ____, ____ new additional net / month

    b.   +   2a $ ____, ____, ____ current net per month

    c.   = $ ____, ____, ____ total new net profit / month

    d. **6c x 12 =** $ ____, ____, ____ **total new net profit per year**

Use the calculator at JoeVerde.com/net7 with your numbers.

DO THE MATH IN EVERY AREA
USING OUR ONLINE CALCULATORS

The quick & easy way to do the math and the other 'what ifs' on what we'll cover in here is to go to JoeVerde.com/calc7 and use our calculators.

We also have other calculators there for you to find out...

1. **What's your *real* advertising cost per unit?**

   Why do I say, your 'real' cost? Because most of us were taught to find ad costs per unit by using a bad formula. I was taught to take our total ad budget and divide it by our total sales, instead of dividing the ad budget by only the sales that came directly from the advertising. How about you?

   Are you ready to see what your ad-generated sales really cost your dealership? If so, take 2 minutes and complete the 'Ad Cost' calculator.

2. **What's the value of setting goals correctly for your dealership?**

   Everyone wants to sell more and earn more, and when you set a goal correctly, it's such a straightforward process, that everyone can increase their sales and income year after year. Unfortunately, most of us weren't taught how to set goals correctly. That's why people miss the first two critical steps of setting goals 97% of the time. (Get everyone a copy of my free "Goal Setting For Salespeople" book at JoeVerde.com/store)

   Take 2 minutes and walk through the math on how to set and reach your sales, profit and growth goals each year.

3. **What do your below average salespeople really cost you each year?**

   "Average" ... The bottom of the top & the top of the bottom.

   10 units per month is average, and anything below 10 is *below average*. Getting all of your salespeople to 15 or 20 would be great, but you don't have to do that for huge increases in your net profit. There is a ton of potential net profit in just taking your 5, 6 and 8 unit salespeople up to average.

   How much potential? To find out, just plug in the numbers for your group, and I guarantee you'll be shocked.

4. **What are your salespeople's individual potential?** There's a calculator just for salespeople, so they can see their long term potential by making even small improvements in their unit sales and gross profit (commission).

Go to ... JoeVerde.com/calc7

Use your own numbers in these calculators. Take just 2 minutes to have some fun, and see how easy and profitable growth really is.

**Is a 15% improvement
in units and gross realistic?**

"We started using Joe's online training 3 months ago, along with having weekly training meetings. We focus on using Joe's word tracks to **overcome objections** and make sure our salespeople **don't skip any steps** in the sales process.

With just those minor changes, we had our **2nd best month in 10 years** and now we're on track for our best year.

Thanks Joe!"

– Jake Sodikoff, General Manager
Steven Kia, Harrisonburg, Virginia

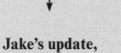

**Jake's update,
just 5 months later...**

"After 8 months training on JVTN® 3 days a week, our volume is up 16% over last year and our gross is already 20% higher than last year.

In addition, we had a record month in September. JVTN® has helped our sales team **overcome objections** on the lot and has helped us **close deals** we never would have had."

– Jake Sodikoff, General Manager
Steven Kia, Harrisonburg, Virginia

Seriously – Slow Down...

We've covered an awful lot so far, and I know you already have dozens of ideas on how you can increase your unit sales, your gross profit, and your net profit – just by improving your salespeople's skills, processes and their work habits.

We'll do a quick review of what we've covered, and then let's dive into those Top 7 Highest Sales and Gross Profit Sources so you can take your dealership to the next level.

Slow down and take 20 minutes to think about what we've covered so far. And take another 20 minutes on each of the 7 solutions we'll cover next.

Tip: No distractions ... No TV, no kids, no dogs, no calls, no texts, no emails.

Just you, this book and your spiral notebook.

A Quick Recap

What have we covered so far that will help you increase your unit sales, your gross profit, and your net profit – without spending any extra money?

1. **Buyers** ... First and most important ... every person on your lot is a buyer, and you absolutely do not need more traffic to increase your sales. Your opportunity to double sales is on your lot, every single month.

    Our sample 100 unit dealership has $1,000,000 in gross profit walking on the lot every month, but $750,000 is doing a u-turn without buying.

    How about you – how many sales and how much gross are you turning away each month because your salespeople lack critical selling skills?

2. **Change** ... I hope I've reminded you that when something isn't working, or when it stops working – that you need to try something different.

    Advertising to try to grow is like that hamster in the cage – it's huffin' and puffin' trying to get somewhere, but it really isn't making any progress. Instead of that circular 'buy ads / price shoppers show / lose almost every sale' track that leads to continuous disappointment, it's time to get on a flat track with no obstacles, so you can set clear goals and achieve them.

3. **You're In The Wrong Line If** ... You're spending way too much time and money on ads, BDCs, leads, etc. and getting minimal, one-shot results at best.

    If you went to the bank and there were two lines; one teller was paying out $2 for every $1 you gave him, and the other was paying $30 to $1, plus regular monthly dividends, which line would you push and shove to get into?

    How long have you been standing in the wrong line, hoping you'd get lucky and that advertising will pay better next time? More important, how much longer will you keep waiting in that small return line?

4. **Good Gross** ... The difference between a 'well' and an 'artesian well' is that with a well, you have to pump and pump forever or you don't get water. An artesian well is under pressure and just keeps pushing water to you.

    Advertising is like that well, you've gotta keep spending money like there's no tomorrow to keep your sales high enough to make a profit.

    When you focus on areas that don't cost you any extra money, like the artesian well, that new skill or process just keeps pushing your profits higher and higher, as long as you keep the valves open so it keeps flowing.

5. **15%** ... No matter how many units you sell, something very close to a 15% increase in units and gross will double your net profit. Do your own math.

If you're ready to start selling more cars, having more fun,
and making a lot more money – let's get started.

Want Results Even Faster? Get Every Manager Involved!

1. Get every manager a copy of this book. You want every manager on board when you start to set your goals and make your plans.

2. Have every manager read this book, add up your dealership numbers, do the math, set a goal and fill in an action plan in each area on what you want to improve.

3. Schedule management meetings to talk about each solution. Have everyone discuss their notes on the opportunities in each area we'll cover, their estimates of your potential to improve, and the steps they feel you need to take to implement your plan.

4. As a group, select <u>one area to focus on for the next 90 days</u> (or until you reach that goal) and as a group, set a realistic goal.

   (Remember, my goal setting book is free: JoeVerde.com/store)

5. Work with your salespeople on that topic every day. It doesn't have to be an hour meeting – just get everyone to *talk* about what they're doing, share their success and where they need more help.

6. Track everything involved in each solution we cover. If it's about selling more to floor traffic – track total ups, demos, write ups (both committed and non-committed write-ups), deliveries, gross, the manager who worked the deal, and source it accurately.

7. At the end of every 30 days, review your progress, adapt and adjust your plan as needed, and focus on the next 30 days.

   Schedule your plans and training for 30 days at a time, and stay focused on that solution until you reach your goal.

If you're on JVTN® – you can take the fast track...

There's a good chance you're on JVTN® now, and that means *you have a complete training course for every topic in this book.* Just follow the directions in each course on the number of meetings to hold, discussion topics for each meeting, practice sessions, and easy spiffs to keep the focus on that activity.

If you aren't on JVTN® now, if you've been through our sales class, or our closing and objection handling workshop for salespeople – or to our desking and negotiation workshop for managers, use your workbooks from those courses as guides to move the needle in every area.

Common Question

"Why Focus On Just One Solution For 90 Days?"

Your goal is *permanent improvement*, not just a quick fix that disappears in a few weeks. Take doing more demos – you can put a $10 spiff on demos for 30 days and double demos. You'll sell a bunch of extra units, do high fives and probably figure you're done, and head to the next solution.

What happens when your focus on demos shifts? Absolutely, the improvement starts sliding back to its previous level. That's why you hear so many managers who focused on a change for only a month say, "Oh, we did that and it was a quick shot in the arm, but it didn't last."

The goal is permanent improvement – so how long does that take?

Change is a 3-stage process, and in class we recommend you give each stage 60 to 90 days of continuous focus. Why? Because your real goal is to make every new change a permanent improvement in how you do business.

Change for permanent improvement happens in these 3 stages...

New Rule & Training	Now It's A Managed Habit	How You Do Business
60 – 90 Days	60 – 90 Days	60 – 90 Days

Change usually starts with a rule like: We want 75% demos. Problem: People don't like change, so your resistance fighters *light the fire*. When that happens, improvements fall apart in most dealerships because the managers and the dealer aren't prepared to overcome the resistance.

Think of change and improvements in 3 stages...

1. New rule ... "We want 75% demos." The first 60 to 90 days, you have to train everyone so they *can do* what you want - and then you have to manage them every day to make sure they *are doing* what you said.

2. It's a habit now, but it still has to be managed. You'll move onto training on some other skill, but you still have to manage demos daily.

3. Your business philosophy ... now the habit is developed, and salespeople and management are doing 75% demos. The resistance fighters are either doing what you said or they left a long time ago.

Stage 3 is critical with every new change because when you hire new salespeople, they'll learn the rules and boundaries in your dealership from what everyone else does, not just from what you put in your procedure manual.

The goal isn't to just 'try something new' with these solutions.
Your goal is to implement training & processes for permanent improvement.

YOUR FIRST 4 SOLUTIONS

4 DIFFERENT WAYS TO
DOUBLE YOUR NET PROFIT
FROM THE FLOOR TRAFFIC
YOU ALREADY HAVE

**A Sample 100 Unit Dealership
We'll Use For All Examples***

Units Per Month 100

Closing / Delivery Ratio 20%

Average Gross Per Unit $2,500

Average Sales & Management Comp. 40%

Annual (Pre-Tax) Net Profit $500,000

---

*Go to JoeVerde.com/net7 to enter your numbers.

FLOOR TRAFFIC

SOLUTION #1

MORE DEMOS = MORE SALES

Most salespeople want to jump on the fast track to the sale and get it over with quick, so they can get another 'up', especially on those busy traffic days.

To save time, one of the most common shortcuts most salespeople take is to skip the demonstration and just try to get the prospect inside as quickly as possible.

The problem with that, and one of the biggest reasons dealerships miss some of the easiest sales is because...

NO DEMO = NO SALE

This Is Only About The 'Number' Of Demos

I'm only talking about increasing the *number of demos* your salespeople give your customers each month.

Of course, a *great* demo is better, but even your worst salesperson will deliver more units just by putting more people behind the wheel.

WHICH OF THESE FACTS AFFECT YOUR
UNIT SALES, GROSS PROFIT & YOUR PAYCHECK?

✍ *Circle the # for each fact that affects your paycheck and fill in the blanks...*

1. **99% of the people will not buy without driving first.**

    ✍ How does this affect our sales and gross profit potential?_____
    _____

    ✍ What are the most common reasons / excuses we hear <u>and accept</u> about why our customers are not getting a demonstration?
    _____
    _____

    ✍ What can we do to insure that every customer not only gets a demo, but that they get a *targeted* demo & presentation of our product?_____
    _____
    _____

    ✍ Which of our salespeople and managers don't understand, or simply ignore the fact that people don't buy vehicles without driving them first?

    _____ _____ _____ _____ _____ _____ _____

    ✍ How much does this cost me personally each month? $_____

2. **80% of both buying and selling happens in the demo and presentation on just 20% of the key Hot Button features the customer cares about most.**

    ✍ How does this affect our sales and gross profit potential?_____
    _____

    ✍ Are our salespeople finding Hot Button features they can 'sell' when they're on the demo, or are they focusing more on price, payments, etc?
    _____

    ✍ Does our selling process and the steps we tell salespeople to follow lead them to focus on value or pricing?_____
    _____

    ✍ Our salespeople focus on pricing when they...
    ❑ Select a Vehicle   ❑ Close   ❑ Get Objections   ❑ Negotiate
    ✍ Which of our managers and salespeople need to improve in this area?

    _____ _____ _____ _____ _____ _____ _____

    ✍ How much does this cost me personally each month? $_____

3. **Buying is 'emotional' and the demonstration is the highest emotional point in the selling process, and it's where a 'targeted' presentation on their Hot Button features creates the highest value.**

✍ How does this fact affect our sales and gross profit potential?_____

_____

✍ Which of our salespeople (and managers) either don't understand, or simply ignore the emotional impact of a demonstration of the vehicle?

_____   _____   _____   _____   _____   _____   _____

✍ What can we do to help them understand the value, or to simply require that they demonstrate our vehicles? _____

_____

_____

✍ How much does this cost me personally each month? $_____

4. **On the demo, the targeted presentations to the Secondary Driver and then to the Primary Driver,** *set up the 4-step closing sequence.*

✍ How does this affect our sales and gross profit potential? _____

_____

✍ Are our salespeople giving their targeted presentations during the demo (the highest emotional point)? _____

_____

_____

✍ Are our presentations 'targeted' to each buyer's Hot Buttons? _____

_____

_____

✍ What % of our demos lead into the 4-step closing process?

10%   20%   30%   40%   50%   60%   70%   80%   90%

✍ What are we doing to encourage (or allow) salespeople to skip the demo, and to just bring the customer inside as soon as possible to start working the deal (on price)? _____

_____

_____

✍ Which of our salespeople need to improve in this area?

_____   _____   _____   _____   _____   _____   _____

✍ How much does this cost me personally each month? $_____

5. **50% of the people who get a *good* demo buy on the spot.**

    ✍ How does this fact affect our sales and gross profit potential?_____

    _____

    ✍ What % of our customers actually get a demo? (Circle one.)
    10% 20% 30% 40% 50% 60% 70% 80% 90%

    ✍ Of the demos our salespeople do give, what % are good to great?
    10% 20% 30% 40% 50% 60% 70% 80% 90%

    ✍ Which of our salespeople need to improve in this area?

    _____ _____ _____ _____ _____ _____ _____

    ✍ What can we do to improve our demo percentage? _____

    _____

    ✍ How much does this cost me personally each month? $_____

6. **99% won't buy without one. 50% do buy when they get a good demo and presentation. Unfortunately, <u>only 40%</u> actually get a demo.**

    From our online survey of 3,500+ salespeople and managers, they admit they only give *4 out of 10 (expensive)* prospects a demo.

    Why are their numbers different than your log sheets?

    Because we ask, "Forget what you put on the log sheet – how many out of every 10 people you talk to on the lot, including service customers who come up front, people on their lunch hour and even kids who say their parents told them to start looking, actually get a demo?"

    (4 out of 10) is always the average. Why count service, lunch hour lookers and kids? Because we've all delivered some of them in the past, but not until they got a demo and presentation. *So count everyone!*

    Caution: Some dealers say, "We're doing 75% demos."

    So far, I've never found even one dealership (that counted everyone who shows an interest in a vehicle) with a real 75% demo rate. Some argued they did, *until they hired a spotter* to count everyone their salespeople talk to. In the end, it's always been closer to 40% than 75%.

    More demos equal more sales for you, too.

    Knowing 50% purchase after they get a good demonstration,
    if you'll do your own math, you'll probably find you're also
    delivering about half the people who get demos now.

HOW TO REALISTICALLY IMPROVE
SALES 50 UNITS & THE NET $900,000

Increase Demos & Deliver More Vehicles

No unrealistic highballs needed ... just demo 6 instead of 4.

Now – At 40% Demos			Improve Demo Ratio To 60%	
500	Prospects		500	Prospects
x 40%	**Demos**		x 60%	**Demos**
200	Demos	→	300	Demos
x 50%	Buy w/good Demo		x 50%	Buy w/good Demo
100	Deliveries	→	150	Deliveries

Your Good Gross Improvement

50	**More units every month**
x $2,500	More in Good Gross per unit
$125,000	Additional Good Gross per month
x 12	Months
$1,500,000	Additional **Good Gross** per year

Double Your Net With More Demos

Your Net Profit Increase

$1,500,000	Additional **Good Gross** per year
x 60%	Good Gross to Net Profit
$75,000	**Additional Net Profit per month**

+ $900,000
Additional **Net Profit** per year

Your Cost To Increase Sales & Net Profit ... $1,270

Double down on demos and you'll double up on sales!

OUR DEMO POTENTIAL

The Potential You See In Your Dealership

1. ✍ As a dealership, how are you doing on demonstrating the vehicle to every customer now? Rate your dealership from 10% - 100%.

$$10\% - 20 - 30 - 40 - 50 - 60 - 70 - 80 - 90 - 100\%$$

Wait! Don't be like most managers in class who use the numbers posted on their log sheet. Why? Because they probably aren't accurate. We're talking real life for this rating, with no fluff.

Counting service customers who look at a vehicle, those 'just lookers', people who try to trade too soon, and even the kids you know who can't buy without approval – how many out of 10 are getting a demonstration?

Be brutally honest in your guesstimate, so you can set a real improvement goal. What's your actual percentage of demos now? _____%

Tip: If you aren't sure on demos, just take your sales volume and double it, and that's about how many demos your salespeople are doing.

✍ If we just got more people behind the wheel of our vehicles each month, **I believe we could sell _____ more units every month.**

2. ✍ **The Math:** If we just did more demos...

    a. From #1, we could realistically sell _____ **more units per mo.**

    b. Using our total sales and F&I gross of $ _____ per unit

    c. 'a' x 'b' would add *good gross* of $ _____,_____ per month

    d. At 60% of 'c' to net, we'd *net an extra* $ _____,_____ per month

    e. In one year, that extra net profit would be $ ___ , _____ , _____

3. ✍ **WIIFM** (What's In It For Me?)

    If we did more demos and sold those extra units every month...

    I'd personally earn an extra $ _____ per month,
    and that means I'd make $ _____ more per year.

For a quick increase in personal income,
just make sure every customer drives a vehicle!

DEMO IMPROVEMENT

My Action Page & 90 Day Goal

1. ✍ List your salespeople who could improve their demo ratios.

   Fill in the number of units they're at now, then write in their realistic potential by improving their # of demos. How many more deliveries would that mean per month?

Salesperson's Name	# Units Now	Improve Demo %	# Extra Units
_____	_____ units	_____ %	_____ / Mo.
_____	_____ units	_____ %	_____ / Mo.
_____	_____ units	_____ %	_____ / Mo.
_____	_____ units	_____ %	_____ / Mo.
_____	_____ units	_____ %	_____ / Mo.
_____	_____ units	_____ %	_____ / Mo.
_____	_____ units	_____ %	_____ / Mo.
_____	_____ units	_____ %	_____ / Mo.
_____	_____ units	_____ %	_____ / Mo.
_____	_____ units	_____ %	_____ / Mo.
_____	_____ units	_____ %	_____ / Mo.
_____	_____ units	_____ %	_____ / Mo.

Total Extra Units For Your Dealership...   **_____ / Mo.**

2. How can you increase your number of demos?

   • **WIIF<u>T</u>** ... Talk to salespeople about *'What's In It For <u>T</u>hem'* to do more demos – more sales, easier sales, more income, more fun.

   • Train and show them how to get more customers behind the wheel.

   • Train and show them how to do more effective 'Hot Button' demos.

   • Create spiffs that tie to the activity you want: More demos.

   Complete your action plan and goals on the next page...

Tip: If you're on JVTN® – go through the course, "How To Sell More Cars Every Month". Check the Leader's Guide on some easy, inexpensive spiff ideas to get them focused on doing more demos – which leads to more sales.

DEMO IMPROVEMENT
My Action Page & 90 Day Goal (Continued)

94% of written goals that include a clear plan are achieved.

3. ✎ My 90 day goal: We will improve our demonstration percentage to ____ % of all of our customers and prospects by ___ / ___ / ___.

4. ✎ The steps we'll take to reach our goal on demonstrations are...

1. _____
   _____
   _____

2. _____
   _____
   _____

3. _____
   _____
   _____

4. _____
   _____
   _____

✓ Create a 'Goals' book for yourself. A simple spiral notebook or 3-ring binder works great.

✓ Get my book, "Goal Setting For Salespeople" for every salesperson and manager. Go to JoeVerde.com/store. It's free.

✓ Tip: Give each manager a small group of salespeople to train, coach and manage to help each salesperson achieve their individual goals.

✓ Tip: Get salespeople and managers to class or on JVTN® and we'll put them on a fast track to improve in every area we cover.

5. Hold a short management meeting each morning on your progress until you've reached your goal.

"Getting ready is the secret of success."

– Henry Ford

✍ Write Out Your Thoughts On Improving
The Quality & Quantity Of Demos In Your Dealership

_____

_____

_____

_____

_____

_____

_____

_____

_____

_____

_____

_____

_____

_____

_____

_____

_____

_____

_____

_____

_____

_____

Once more, so you don't forget...

"Double down on demos – and you'll double up on sales!"

That's an accurate statement – so write down everything you're
thinking right now about how you can improve your demos and sales.

*"Luck is what happens
when preparation meets opportunity."*
– Seneca, 65 AD

You'll find that you get lucky more often
when you focus as much time on improving your
selling process and your salespeople's skills
as you do trying to generate more leads.

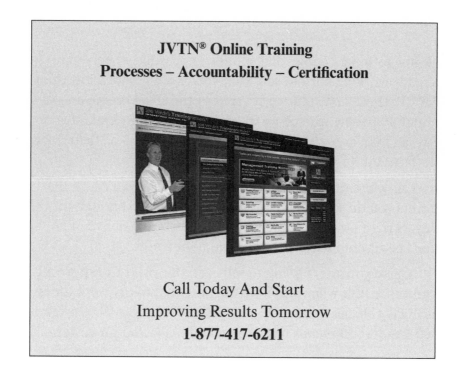

JVTN® Online Training

Processes – Accountability – Certification

Call Today And Start
Improving Results Tomorrow
1-877-417-6211

FLOOR TRAFFIC
SOLUTION #2

IMPROVE THE
SELLING PROCESS

Is doubling your unit sales possible?

I know to some people, that sounds impossible when you're already working hard to sell what you're selling now. But think back to those first stats we covered or the chart on buyers – 8 out of 10 people who come to your dealership to look, do buy, and the average dealership delivers just 20% of their floor traffic (2 out of 10).

In reality, use those two stats or just look at the chart on the buyers you do sell – you'll see that there are still enough unsold buyers right now for that 100 unit dealership to deliver 400 units per month with no additional floor traffic.

Of course you aren't going to sell everyone on your lot, we all know that. But when you have the potential to deliver 4 times as many vehicles as you are now, selling 20%-30%-50% or even 100% more just means improving your skills and processes.

More importantly, you can easily increase your sales volume, your gross and your net profit year after year, without spending any more money on more ads, marketing or leads.

WHICH OF THESE FACTS ABOUT 'SELLING' AFFECT YOUR PAYCHECK?

Facts About The 3-Stage Selling Process...
Warm Up → Build Value → Close

✍ *Circle the # for each fact that affects your paycheck and fill in the blanks...*

1. **95%+ of the people have done some research online.**

   ✍ How does this fact affect our sales and gross profit potential?_____
   _____

2. **8 out of 10 people who come into the dealership will buy.**

   ✍ How does this fact affect our sales and gross profit potential?_____
   _____
   _____

3. **71% buy because they like their salesperson and the process.**

   ✍ How does this fact affect our sales and gross profit potential?_____
   _____

   ✍ Which costs us sales – and why?
   ❑ We lack a clear process on building rapport
   ❑ We have a process, but don't require salespeople to follow it_____
   ❑ We don't train effectively

   ✍ Explain: _____
   _____

   ✍ Which of our salespeople and managers need to improve in this area?

   _____ _____ _____ _____ _____ _____ _____

4. **71% who didn't buy, found a vehicle they would have purchased, but didn't – because they didn't like the salesperson or the process.**

   ✍ How does this fact affect our sales and gross profit potential?_____
   _____

   ✍ What causes this problem, and what more can we do to prevent this from costing us sales? _____
   _____
   _____

   ✍ How much does this cost me personally each month? $_____

5. **85% said their salesperson didn't build rapport.**

✍ How does this fact affect our sales and gross profit potential?_____
_____

✍ What are we doing / not doing that causes us to lose sales because our salespeople aren't building rapport (or don't know how), which is critical to creating the 'like' that usually makes or breaks most sales?
_____
_____

✍ Which of our salespeople and managers need to build more rapport?

_____ _____ _____ _____ _____ _____ _____

✍ How much does this cost me personally each month? $_____

6. **80% of buying & selling is on just 20% of the features. (Each different customer's Hot Buttons).**

✍ How does this affect our sales and gross profit potential?_____
_____

✍ How are our salespeople really doing at finding Hot Buttons, and then pushing them to generate the value needed to make the sale? _____
_____
_____

✍ Which of our salespeople and managers need to <u>find</u> Hot Buttons?

_____ _____ _____ _____ _____ _____ _____

✍ How much does this cost me personally each month? $_____

7. **85% said their salesperson didn't find out what was important to them. (Those Hot Buttons again).**

✍ How does this fact affect our sales and gross profit potential?_____
_____

✍ Can they, and are our salespeople finding Hot Buttons? ❑ Yes ❑ No
✍ If not, why not?_____
_____

✍ Which of our salespeople & managers need to focus on pushing Hot Buttons?

_____ _____ _____ _____ _____ _____ _____

✍ How much does this cost me personally each month? $_____

8. **88% of customers said their presentation and demo (when they got one) were not *targeted* to their specific wants, needs and Hot Buttons.**

✍ How does this fact affect our sales and gross profit potential?_____

_____

✍ Is this from... ❏ Poor Skills   ❏ Poor Process   ❏ Other _____

✍ Explain_____

_____

✍ Which salespeople & managers need to improve presentations & demos?

_____ _____ _____ _____ _____ _____ _____

✍ How much does this cost me personally each month? $_____

9. **8 out of 10 sales are made after salespeople successfully handle or overcome an average of 5 non-price buying objections.**

✍ How does this fact affect our sales and gross profit potential?_____

_____

✍ How well prepared are our salespeople and managers to deal with a customer's buying objections that are not price related? _____

_____

✍ How prepared are our salespeople and managers to deal with *real* price objections they get each day? *Circle one.* 1–2–3–4–5–6–7–8–9–10

✍ Which of our salespeople and managers need to improve in this area?

_____ _____ _____ _____ _____ _____ _____

✍ How much does this cost me personally each month? $_____

10. **75% of salespeople only know one (price related) closing question / objection method, and 75% only ask one time.**

✍ How does this affect our sales and gross profit potential?_____

_____

✍ If salespeople only know one closing question and only ask one time, does that help us make more sales, or does it cost us sales? _____

✍ What can we do to improve in this area? _____

_____

_____

✍ Which of our salespeople and managers need more closing skills?

_____ _____ _____ _____ _____ _____ _____

✍ How much does this cost me personally each month? $_____

11. **Closing and the 'wrap up' to start the paperwork is a 4-step process that begins at the very end of the demonstration.**

✍ How does this fact affect our sales and gross profit potential?_____
_____

✍ Do our salespeople follow a consistent closing process, or just wing it?
_____

✍ What can we do to improve our closing process?_____
_____

✍ Which salespeople & managers don't have a closing & wrap up process?

_____   _____   _____   _____   _____   _____   _____

✍ How much does this cost me personally each month? $_____

12. **"Speed Kills Selling". Closing ratios are 6% when salespeople spend less than 60 minutes *on the lot* with a customer, 31% at 72 minutes, and 57% when they spend 100 minutes or more.**

✍ How does this affect our sales and gross profit potential? _____
_____

✍ On average, our salespeople spend ____ minutes with a customer before they get a commitment to purchase and bring them inside.

✍ 'Quality of the time spent' is certainly important, too. Our salespeople are (circle one) great / good / average / below average ... in selling and closing.

Which of our salespeople & managers try to rush the sale?

_____   _____   _____   _____   _____   _____   _____

✍ How much does this cost me personally each month? $_____

13. **The average delivery ratio from all sources is 20% (2 out of 10), and the reasons it's so low, lies in the facts we just covered.**

✍ How does this affect our sales and gross profit potential? _____
_____

✍ Which of our salespeople & managers need to improve in these areas?

_____   _____   _____   _____   _____   _____   _____

✍ How much does this cost me personally each month? $_____

Why is it so easy to sell more?

Since 8 out of 10 people on the lot specifically came to buy,
how hard can it be to deliver 1 or 2 more of the 6 that were missed?

✍ What 'Profit Potential' Opportunities Did You Discover?

1. Go back and highlight the 5 most important facts/stats you see that offer your dealership the greatest potential to improve.

2. Write out your 'off the cuff' first thoughts about how you can improve in each of those 5 areas. List the fact # and your thoughts.

\# _____ _____

_____

\# _____ _____

_____

\# _____ _____

_____

\# _____ _____

_____

\# _____ _____

_____

✍ Other Ideas You Have On Improving Your Sales Process

_____

_____

_____

_____

_____

_____

_____

_____

_____

_____

_____

_____

_____

_____

_____

_____

How To Realistically Improve
Sales 50 Units & The Net $900,000

Improve Your Selling Skills And Selling Processes

No need for unrealistic highballs … just improve your actual closing ratio from 20% to 30% by developing your salespeople's selling skills, and you'll easily increase your deliveries by 50%.

Sales Now – Closing At 20%			Improve Closing Ratio To 30%	
500	Prospects		500	Prospects
x 20%	**Closing Ratio**		x 30%	**Closing Ratio**
100	Deliveries	→	150	Deliveries

Your Good Gross Improvement

50	**More units every month**
x $2,500	More in Good Gross per unit
$125,000	Additional Good Gross per month
x 12	Months
$1,500,000	Additional **Good Gross** per year

Double Your Net With Better Selling Skills

Your Net Profit Increase

$1,500,000	Additional **Good Gross** per year
x 60%	Good Gross to Net Profit
$75,000	**Additional Net Profit per month**

+ $900,000
Additional **Net Profit** per year

Your Cost To Increase Sales & Net Profit … $1,270

SALESPEOPLE LACK CORE SKILLS

What Is Their Skill Level Now?

We've surveyed over 3,500 salespeople online, and thousands more in our classes. From their responses, 80% didn't receive enough training to even become average, much less to become high achievers.

• Fast Food Employees ... Offer a $1-$5 product. Workers earn around $9 to $10 per hour, get one to two weeks *plus* of 1-1 training initially with a team leader, and ongoing training and review the rest of their career.

• Automotive Salespeople ... Sell a $25,000-$100,000 product with unlimited variations in models, colors & equipment, who must handle an average of 5 non-price buying objections, and just as many equally difficult price issues, and then negotiate a win/win to deliver a vehicle.

Training ... Automotive Salespeople surveyed said they got 7.4 hours of initial training when they started, and 80% of the training was on product, not on how to sell. They rated their initial training a 4 out of 10 and 80% said they got no further *sales* training. That's one reason 82% of new hires are history within 6 months, and why 80% who stay become *just average* or below average salespeople.

> Average automobile salespeople deliver 10 units
> per month or less, and earn +/– $40,000 per year.
>
> High achievers deliver 20 to 100+ units per
> month, and earn $100,000 to $400,000 per year.

In 30+ years, we've helped develop most of the highest achievers in sales, in sales management, and today's dealers by giving them the training and processes they would have never received without our training.

The differences between average salespeople and high achievers fall into 4 key areas that control everyone's success in sales. In class, we refer to these as SHAC...

- **Skills** ... Higher achievers obviously have higher skill levels in sales.

- **Habits** ... They go to work 'to work' and are productive the entire day doing something to either sell now or to generate a sale in the future.

- **Attitude** ... All high achievers have a positive attitude about selling and success and are successful because they expect to succeed.

- **Choice Of Customers** ... High achievers develop their own customer base and make most of their sales to repeat customers, service customers, referrals and prospects they bring into the dealership. They do not focus on the hard to close, price shopping 'walk-in' customers dealers provide.

When you're ready to develop and retain your own high achievers, get managers to our management course, and get everyone to our sales classes.

CORE SKILLS SALESPEOPLE NEED

A Common Misunderstanding On
Processes vs. Skills

Processes ... A process is made up of the *steps* you take to complete something, whether it's building a house, selling a car, or prospecting out in service.

Common processes your salespeople need...

- How to sell the vehicle – how to close the sale – how to 'work a deal'
- How to turn a call or internet lead into an appointment, then a delivery
- How to prospect for new business in service and in their customer base
- How to follow up & get unsold customers back in, who just left
- How to follow up sold customers immediately, then how to retain forever
- And everything else you want or need salespeople to do. Every task is process based. That's why having effective processes is critical.

Every process above is different, because each process has a different goal. The *8 Step Process To Sell A Car* is different than the *6 Steps To Turn A Call Into An Appointment That Shows,* which is different than the *3 Steps To Prospect* to find the next buyer in the family.

Here's where the confusion comes in on processes and skills...

The 3 Core Selling Skills ... The steps in each process are different, but the core selling skills required for each process **are the same** and fall into 3 main categories. That's why you'll hear us say, *"Phone skills are not a different set of skills, they're just selling skills you use when you have a phone in your hand."*

- **Asking Questions** is a critical core skill in every process above.
- **Dealing With Price** on the lot, when closing, in the negotiation, in taking calls, in follow up and responding to leads, is another core skill.
- **Selling Skills** like closing, building value, overcoming objections, and negotiating are critical skills salespeople need in every process.

To use incoming calls, for example ...

If a salesperson doesn't know how, and can't ask the *right questions* to control the conversation and get information on the lot, they can't on the phone either. If they don't understand how to *handle price* effectively on the lot, they can't on the phone. And if they don't know how to *sell* to build value, overcome objections and close the sale on the lot, they sure can't sell, overcome objections or close on an appointment on the phone either.

The success you want most comes from the core skills your salespeople lack.

Rate Each Salesperson's Selling Skills (1-10)   List salespeople, score each area, then find 'average'.

30 Ways To Improve Sales & Gross *List their names at the right, rate each salesperson in every category below and find their 'averages'.*											Totals	Average
QUESTIONS												
1. 'Yes' Questions: Ties Down Benefits / Commitments												
2. Open Ended Questions: Builds Rapport												
3. 'Either / Or' Questions: Controls – Investigates – Closes												
PRICE: QUESTIONS – CONCERNS – OBJECTIONS												
4. Bypasses Price On Lot & Focuses On Value												
5. Rephrases Price When Closing												
6. Refocuses Price In Negotiation												
SELLING PROCESS												
7. Correct Greeting To Get Name & Control												
8. Builds Rapport												
9. Investigates To Find Customer HOT BUTTONS												
10. Service: Sells People & Value												
11. Control: Keeps The Sale Moving Forward												
12. Selects Best Vehicle On HOT BUTTONS – Not Price												
13. Demo: Salesperson Drives 1st & Covers FABs												
14. Targeted Pres. & Demo To Secondary & Primary Driver												
15. Starts Closing Now With 5 to 7 Summary 'Yes' Questions												
16. Assumptive 'Sold Line' & 'Either / Or' Closing Question												
17. Gets 6 To 12 Action Closing Commitments												
18. Silent Trade Walk Around W/MPG & Maintenance Info												
19. Wrap Up & Final 'Either / Or' Close To Move Inside												
20. Negotiation: Properly Sets Up & Gets First Signature												
21. Completes Req. Paperwork B4 Negotiation Starts												
22. Gets Committed Buyers On All Write Ups												
23. Negotiation: Rate 3-Pass Process, Overall...												
24. Works Terms (Down & Payment) Not Price												
25. Maintains Control In The Negotiation												
26. Effective W/Gas Saving & Maintenance Closes												
27. Effectively & Correctly Transitions To Finance												
CLOSING ON OBJECTIONS												
28. Uses 'Seriously Now' In Closing & Negotiation												
29. Uses 'Agree & Close' In Closing & Negotiation												
30. Uses CRIC: Clarify – Rephrase – Isolate – Close												
Total Scores												

Selling Skills Control Every Area You Need
To Improve In To Sell More & Earn More

✍ You rated your salespeople on 'selling on the lot'. Now, make a copy of this page for each salesperson and circle their skill level on these 3 processes.

Salesperson's Name:_____

Unsold Follow Up

Getting Contact Information	1 – 2 – 3 – 4 – 5 – 6 – 7 – 8 – 9 – 10
Making The Contact	1 – 2 – 3 – 4 – 5 – 6 – 7 – 8 – 9 – 10
Bypassing / Rephrasing Price	1 – 2 – 3 – 4 – 5 – 6 – 7 – 8 – 9 – 10
Handling Common Objections	1 – 2 – 3 – 4 – 5 – 6 – 7 – 8 – 9 – 10
Getting Firm Appointments That Show	1 – 2 – 3 – 4 – 5 – 6 – 7 – 8 – 9 – 10

Incoming Sales Calls

Quickly Controlling The Call	1 – 2 – 3 – 4 – 5 – 6 – 7 – 8 – 9 – 10
Bypassing / Rephrasing Price	1 – 2 – 3 – 4 – 5 – 6 – 7 – 8 – 9 – 10
Handling Common Objections	1 – 2 – 3 – 4 – 5 – 6 – 7 – 8 – 9 – 10
Getting Contact Information	1 – 2 – 3 – 4 – 5 – 6 – 7 – 8 – 9 – 10
Getting Firm Appointments That Show	1 – 2 – 3 – 4 – 5 – 6 – 7 – 8 – 9 – 10

Prospecting In Person & By Phone

Building Rapport Quickly	1 – 2 – 3 – 4 – 5 – 6 – 7 – 8 – 9 – 10
Controlling The Conversation	1 – 2 – 3 – 4 – 5 – 6 – 7 – 8 – 9 – 10
Finding The Next Buyer In Their Family	1 – 2 – 3 – 4 – 5 – 6 – 7 – 8 – 9 – 10
Service Cust: Getting Them To Look Now	1 – 2 – 3 – 4 – 5 – 6 – 7 – 8 – 9 – 10
Phone: Getting Firm Appointments	1 – 2 – 3 – 4 – 5 – 6 – 7 – 8 – 9 – 10

Which of the processes rely on the same 3 skills we just covered: asking questions, handling price, and their selling skills? Exactly. Your success in every process relies on their skills in those 3 Core Subjects.

Did you know...

The average dealership **can't spend as much** on our training **in a year** to potentially **double sales** – as they **spend on advertising each month** just to try to **maintain** their current sales level.

Read that one more time – it's important to your growth.

SELLING SKILLS POTENTIAL

What's The Potential Good Gross Improvement You See?

1. ✍ <u>Complete</u> the Rating Sheet, <u>then list</u> all of your salespeople who could sell more by improving their selling skills and <u>write in</u> what you see as a realistic improvement for that salesperson.

Salesperson	Improvement	Salesperson	Improvement
_____	by + ___ units	_____	by + ___ units
_____	by + ___ units	_____	by + ___ units
_____	by + ___ units	_____	by + ___ units
_____	by + ___ units	_____	by + ___ units
_____	by + ___ units	_____	by + ___ units
_____	by + ___ units	_____	by + ___ units
_____	by + ___ units	_____	by + ___ units
_____	by + ___ units	_____	by + ___ units
_____	by + ___ units	_____	by + ___ units
_____	by + ___ units	_____	by + ___ units

Total improvement from all of your salespeople... + _____ Units

2. ✍ **The Math:** If your salespeople improved their core selling skills...

   a. From #1, we could realistically sell   _____ **more units per mo.**

   b. Using our total sales and F&I gross of $ _____ per unit

   c. 'a' x 'b' would add *good gross* of $ _____,_____ per month

   d. At 60% of 'c' to net, we'd *net an extra* $ _____,_____ per month

   e. In one year, that extra net profit would be $ ___ , _____ , _____

3. ✍ **WIIFM** (What's In It For Me?) If we did a better job of selling and delivered those extra units every month...

   I'd personally earn an extra $ _____ per month,

   and that means I'd make $ _____ more per year.

SELLING SKILLS
My Action Page & 90 Day Goal

1. Tip: Have every manager rate each salesperson, then compare notes. Everyone will have different ideas on each salesperson's potential, but in the end you want to make sure all managers are on the same page about what needs to be done to start improving each person right away.

2. ✍ My 90 day goal: We'll improve our *90 day unit sales average* from _____ units per month to _____ units per month by ___ / ___ / ___.

   Read my book, "Goal Setting For Salespeople" to see how to improve your salespeople's current averages instead of just working with their month to month sales. It's free at JoeVerde.com.

3. ✍ The steps we'll take to reach our goals are...

   1. _____
      _____

   2. _____
      _____

   3. _____
      _____

   4. _____
      _____

   ✓ Tip: Create a 'goals' book for yourself. A simple spiral notebook or 3 ring binder works great.

   ✓ Tip: Give each manager a small group of salespeople to train, coach and manage to help each salesperson achieve their individual goals.

   ✓ Tip: Get every manager to our "Sales Management Boot Camp".

4. To improve sales, gross, and profit...hold a short management meeting each morning on your progress, until you reach your goal.

> *"Sales and profits are missed from a lack of effective processes, daily training and daily management – not from a lack of floor traffic." – Joe Verde*

✍ **Write Out Your Newest Thoughts**
On The Potential You're Starting To See

_____

_____

_____

_____

_____

_____

_____

_____

_____

_____

_____

_____

_____

_____

_____

_____

_____

_____

_____

_____

_____

_____

_____

Thinking is the hardest thing for most people to do.

When you remember how to daydream with a purpose, and discipline
yourself to make the time regularly – you can accomplish anything.

"I feel like a kid in a candy store!"

We were covering these solutions in class and a manager said, "I feel like a kid in a candy store, and I can't wait to get started!"

If you feel that way too, then it's even more important to slow down long enough to take really good notes and list what you feel is your potential.

To make it happen, compare notes with the other managers in your next management meeting, so you can all focus on the same solution at the same time, with the same plan of attack.

Order your personal key to the candy store today.
Call us now at 1-877-417-6211.

"From 5 units to 17 and double commissions with JVTN®."

"I have been in the car business for 6 months. Prior to this, I was in the restaurant business, working a lot of hours for not a lot of pay.

I've been training on JVTN® since day one. My first month, I sold 5 and my commission average was $300 per unit.

Now 5 months later, by following **Joe's basics**, by mastering **CRIC** and overcoming objections, I am at 17 cars and I have **doubled my commission** to $600 per unit!

I have truly found a profession that has given me untapped potential for all the effort I put forth! Thanks Joe!"

– Michael Wilson, Salesperson
Sierra Blanca Motors, Ruidoso, New Mexico

That's A $400,000 Per Year Increase – Per Salesperson!

Core Skills = More Sales

By improving their **Core Selling Skills,**
each of these salespeople **increased** the 'good gross'
in their dealerships by over **$400,000** per year.

"From 6.5 to 20 units per month with Joe's training!"

"I have been in the car business for 5 months and thanks to Joe Verde and JVTN®, I am the top salesperson in my store!

Having never sold a car before, I was so lucky to be at a dealership that offered real training. I have been training on JVTN® (Joe Verde Training Network®) regularly and after recently attending Joe's 2-Day Sales Workshop, it all came together.

I went from selling 6.5 cars, to 15 cars, then to 20. My gross has been getting better with every vehicle I sell. I've learned how to **stay off price with Joe's 3-step process,** build more **value** with his **steps to the sale**, and most importantly, to stay out of the huddle.

I love JVTN® because it gets me in the right attitude that they are all buyers! It also gives me the 'How-To's' to become a professional in sales and earn $100K. Thanks Joe!"

– Lance Horner, Salesperson
Brinson Ford-Lincoln, Athens, Texas

**"From just 4 units a <u>month</u>,
to 5 units the <u>first week</u> with JVTN®."**

"Since we started JVTN®, we've been training every day, both as a group and individually. Before I did anything else, I made it a point to take my new guys aside and practice some of the **basics** with them: we've been working on moving the sale forward by practicing the **greeting** and **bypassing price.**

We're barely one week into the training, and it has already paid off. A new salesperson who's been with me for 3 months sold 4 cars last month. But as of yesterday, he already has 5 on the board for this month, and it's only into week one!

At this rate, his improvement this month alone will cover my store's entire year of JVTN®!"

*– Rick Wilson, General Manager
Driver's World, Virginia Beach, Virginia*

Zach told us...

"I increased my commissions $250 per unit!"

"I can't thank my manager enough for sending me to your Sales Workshop. Before the class I was averaging 13.6 cars per month, which isn't bad, but I wanted more and needed a clear plan.

I learned how to **slow** the deal **down** and build more **value**, **stay off price**, and most importantly, how to **follow** all of the **8 steps** to the sale (which includes demos).

It definitely worked…I increased my commissions by **$250 per unit, increased my units as well**, and took home a trophy for being in the top 5 salespeople in our group of 11 dealerships.

The timing was perfect because I needed a nice down payment for my new home. Joe, thanks for the tools to make me a sales professional and also for helping make my goal of home ownership a reality!"

– Zach Vogtritter, Salesperson
Springfield Auto Mart, Springfield, Vermont

Results For Zach's Dealership...

$250,000
More Good Gross In Just One Year

$250 more in commission per unit probably means $1,000 more in gross per unit for Zach's dealership.

By being in the top 5 for his group, that's gotta be close to $250,000 *more* good gross profit per year for his dealership, from just one salesperson.

FLOOR TRAFFIC
SOLUTION #3

RAISE THE GROSS
ON EVERY UNIT YOU SELL

Customers definitely ask price questions and they certainly have price concerns about fitting a new vehicle into their budget. Once those questions and concerns are addressed effectively, price falls to the side and isn't anywhere on their list of most important concerns when buying a vehicle.

When you're working a deal, most salespeople and managers let *price* become the focus, but *budget* is, and always has been the real issue – because if they can't come up with the down and they can't afford the payments, there is no deal – no matter how much you discount your vehicle.

Price problems come up when a customer's questions and concerns aren't handled correctly on the lot. Then even the easiest of concerns will quickly become price objections, and those objections will definitely carry over into your negotiation.

Raising the gross *some* on a deal here and there is easy. Raising the gross *significantly* across the board, on every deal, requires an effective, simple, repeatable process, and it requires continuous salesperson and sales management training.

Handling price effectively on the lot is great, but the game changes as soon as desking a deal falls back to 'old school' and becomes a price negotiation.

WHICH OF THESE FACTS
AFFECT YOUR PAYCHECK?

✍ *Circle the # for each fact that affects your paycheck and fill in the blanks...*

1. **Buying is *emotional*, negotiation (price) is *logical*. Passion and desire give way to the logic of down, payments, rates, trade values and payoffs when the conversation turns to price.**

    No matter where you are in the process, once that switch happens, the sale gets tougher.

    ✍ How does this affect our sales and gross profit potential?_____
    _____

    ✍ If 'price' makes it tougher, what are some things we do to cause that?
    _____
    _____
    _____

    ✍ Which of our salespeople or managers need to improve in this area, so we can improve sales & gross?

    _____ _____ _____ _____ _____ _____ _____

    _____ _____ _____ _____ _____ _____ _____

    ✍ How much does this cost me personally each month? $_____

2. **71% buy because they like their salesperson. That's one key reason gross is 40% higher on repeat and referrals than it is for walk-ins.**

    ✍ How does this affect our sales and gross profit potential?_____
    _____
    _____

    ✍ What are we doing that makes 'liking us' tougher? _____
    _____
    _____
    _____

    ✍ Which of our salespeople or managers need to improve in this area, so we can improve sales & gross?

    _____ _____ _____ _____ _____ _____ _____

    _____ _____ _____ _____ _____ _____ _____

    ✍ How much does this cost me personally each month? $_____

3. **M.I.T. proved the importance of 'like' when they found people pay a trusted source 8.1% more.**

On a $20,000 vehicle, 8.1% translates into $1,620 more – which would put it close to the full asking price.

✐ How does this fact affect our sales and gross profit potential?_____
_____

✐ Do our new customers see us as a 'trusted source'? ❏ Yes ❏ No
_____

✐ If 'no' or 'maybe not', what are some of the things we do that can cause that distrust? _____
_____
_____
_____

✐ Which of our salespeople or managers need to improve in this area so we can improve sales & gross?

_____ _____ _____ _____ _____ _____ _____

_____ _____ _____ _____ _____ _____ _____

✐ How much does this cost me personally each month? $_____

4. **16% of buyers pay full price & 30% pay what they're asked to pay.**

(Too bad 'full price' isn't what they're asked to pay more often.)

✐ How does this affect our sales and gross profit potential?_____
_____
_____

✐ What are some processes we have now, or things we do when we're working a deal that actually prevent us from asking for full price?

• Do we ask for full price? _____

• Do we explain why, and defend the price we ask for when we get an objection, or do we just start trying to drop, split, and drop some more? __
_____
_____

✐ Which of our salespeople or managers need to improve in this area, so we can improve sales & gross?

_____ _____ _____ _____ _____ _____ _____

_____ _____ _____ _____ _____ _____ _____

✐ How much does this cost me personally each month? $_____

5. **Price didn't even make the cut in JD Power's 'Top 10' Buyer Survey.**
   More important concerns in order were:

   Reliability – Comfort – Styling – Mileage – Quality
   Convenience – Performance – Technology – Image – Safety

   ✎ How does this affect our sales and gross profit potential?_____

   _____

   ✎ Do we just get the only customers who didn't take the survey above, or are we creating our own price problem on most deals?_____

   _____

   _____

   ✎ What are some things we do to create a price focus, even when the customer cares more about their Hot Buttons?_____

   _____

   _____

   _____

   ✎ Which of our salespeople or managers need to improve in this area, so we can improve sales & gross?

   _____ _____ _____ _____ _____ _____ _____

   _____ _____ _____ _____ _____ _____ _____

   ✎ How much does this cost me personally each month? $_____

6. **Even after the customer finds a vehicle in our inventory, <u>price is still #16</u>. The first 15 on the vehicle are model, color, equipment and other wants & needs.**

   ✎ How does this fact affect our sales and gross profit potential?_____

   _____

   ✎ Since price wasn't even in the top 10, how does our focusing on price throughout the process cost us sales & gross? _____

   _____

   _____

   _____

   ✎ Which of our salespeople or managers need to improve in this area so we can improve sales & gross?

   _____ _____ _____ _____ _____ _____ _____

   _____ _____ _____ _____ _____ _____ _____

   ✎ How much does this cost me personally each month? $_____

7. **The average 'first discount'** *by a salesperson* **within minutes is $844. By the time they start the deal, the discount is up to $2,062.**

✍ How does this affect our sales and gross profit potential?_____
_____

✍ What are some things we do in management to allow, or encourage our salespeople to even discuss discounting price before they have the customer on a vehicle they are ready to purchase?_____
_____
_____
_____

✍ Which of our salespeople or managers need to improve in this area so we can improve sales & gross?

_____ _____ _____ _____ _____ _____ _____

_____ _____ _____ _____ _____ _____ _____

✍ How much does this cost me personally each month? $_____

8. **96% of the customers who are given what they feel is 'the price' (price, trade value, down, payments, etc.) on the lot – who have not committed to purchase first – shop the price.**

Plus, 96% will also shop your price when they feel they've been given 'the price' over the phone or in response to an internet lead – they're going to shop the price you've given them.

That means tossing out a high or low price hook on the lot or on the phone just hoping they'll bite, is 'sales suicide' 96% of the time.

✍ How does this affect our sales and gross profit potential? _____
_____

✍ What are some things we're doing in sales and management to allow, or encourage our salespeople to 'work the deal' on the lot, or to work a deal inside to 'final' figures when we don't have a commitment?
_____
_____
_____

✍ Which of our salespeople or managers need to improve in this area, so we can improve sales & gross?

_____ _____ _____ _____ _____ _____ _____

_____ _____ _____ _____ _____ _____ _____

✍ How much does this cost me personally each month? $_____

9. A 'Good Deal' is a feeling – not a number.

It's a fact – customers who pay the highest gross give you the highest Satisfaction Scores. Why? Because they *feel better* about their purchase.

✍ How does this fact affect our sales and gross profit potential?_____

_____

✍ What are some things we're doing now that keep the focus of our sale and negotiation on price instead of on value?_____

_____

✍ Which of our salespeople or managers need to improve in this area so we can improve sales & gross?   _____ _____ _____ _____

_____ _____ _____ _____ _____ _____ _____

_____ _____ _____ _____ _____ _____ _____

_____ _____ _____ _____ _____ _____ _____

_____ _____ _____ _____ _____ _____ _____

✍ How much does this cost me personally each month? $_____

Why the extra spaces above for 'who' needs to reduce their focus on price? Because most salespeople and managers have a career habit of focusing on price in the selling process, and relying on price to help close the sale.

"Units are up 29%, gross is up 71% from your classes & JVTN®."

"Hello Joe – We've been training in your classes and on JVTN® since 2011. This year (2014) we switched our JVTN® meetings to your recommended **controlled roll out** method, and wow, what a difference it has made!

We train Mon-Wed-Fri and all of our managers do one-on-ones daily with our salespeople, using your Sales Planners. Now we can focus on and practice exactly what we need to take our store to the next level.

It's been incredible! We realized a **29% increase in our units** this year from 565 to 725 and more importantly, we took our **gross up an incredible $711,347 for a 71% increase** this year!

Joe, it's not magic … but having a **clear plan** for the day, week, month, and the year – and having the **proper tools** to execute that plan is the stuff dreams are made of. Thanks for that plan to continue to take our store and our group to the next level!"

– Brian Nesbitt, General Manager
Fred Beans CDJ, Doylestown, PA

How To Realistically Improve
The Net Profit $486,000

Did you know that one of the easiest ways
to increase the net, is to simply raise your gross per unit?

Stop talking price long enough to build value, and raise the gross 25%...

After salespeople and managers take our PRICE course on JVTN® or go to our How To Sell A Car Workshop – they're shocked when they get in front of a customer at just *how easy it is to avoid all the price drama* when they do what they learned, as they watch their gross (commissions) go through the roof.

No magic here, either. In class and on JVTN® we teach your salespeople how to...

- *Bypass* price on the lot to get it out of the conversation, so they can build value.

- *Rephrase* price to budget when they're closing for a commitment.

- *Refocus* price & trade allowance to the 'out of pocket' terms (down & payment) when they're working the deal, instead of grinding out the deal on price & trade, and then still having to work out a payment.

This is so easy because people aren't buying 'price', and in real life, over 90% of the deals you work hinge on 'out of pocket' budget.

$2,500	Total gross PVR now
+ 25%	Increase in gross
= $675	Total gross
x 100	Units now
$67,500	**Additional 'Good Gross' per month** ($675 x 100)

Stop Talking Price And Double Your Net	
$810,000	**Additional Good Gross Per Year**
x 60%	Good Gross To Net
$486,000	**Additional Net Profit Per Year**

Your Cost To Increase Sales & Net Profit ... $1,270

I hope you're seeing that there are plenty of
'Good Gross' opportunities just about everywhere you look.

SKILLS THAT AFFECT GROSS

✍ **Circle The Skills That Affect Sales & Gross**

Selling the vehicle and / or raising the gross
involves each of the 3 Core Skills we covered earlier.

Rate the dealership and then on a separate sheet – rate each person.

1. Price is *not most important* and salespeople and managers have to stop making it the primary focus, even when the customer doesn't.

   As a dealership, do we focus on price – or on value?

   Price ... 1 – 2 – 3 – 4 – 5 – 6 – 7 – 8 – 9 – 10 ... Value

   Why? _____

   _____

2. To earn the customer's confidence, salespeople and managers have to know how to ask questions to quickly build rapport.

   As a dealership, do we talk & talk – or build rapport?

   Talk & Talk ... 1 – 2 – 3 – 4 – 5 – 6 – 7 – 8 – 9 – 10 ... Build Rapport

   Why? _____

   _____

3. Salespeople have to ask questions to find each person's *Hot Button wants and needs* and select a vehicle based on those Hot Buttons instead of price.

   As a dealership, do we focus on price – or do we find their Hot Buttons?

   Price ... 1 – 2 – 3 – 4 – 5 – 6 – 7 – 8 – 9 – 10 ... Hot Buttons

   Why? _____

   _____

4. Salespeople have to know how to *bypass* price (with questions) to move the conversation away from price and get back to features and benefits.

   As a dealership, do we focus on bypassing price – or talk price?

   Talk Price ... 1 – 2 – 3 – 4 – 5 – 6 – 7 – 8 – 9 – 10 ... Bypass Price

   Why? _____

   _____

5. When salespeople close and get a price concern or objection, they have to know how to ask the right questions to *rephrase* price to budget.

   As a dealership, do we focus on dropping price – or rephrasing price?

   Drop Price ... 1 – 2 – 3 – 4 – 5 – 6 – 7 – 8 – 9 – 10 ... Rephrase

   Why? _____

   _____

6. Salespeople have to know how to ask questions to demonstrate, present and target the customer's Hot Button features, instead of just talking discounts, payments and what they think their trade is worth.

   As a dealership, do we focus on price – or do we target Hot Buttons?

   Price ... 1 – 2 – 3 – 4 – 5 – 6 – 7 – 8 – 9 – 10 ... Hot Buttons

   Why? _____

   _____

7. Salespeople have to know how to start the non-price closing process in Step 5 by asking a half dozen benefit summary questions.

   As a dealership, do we focus on price closing – or on a closing process?

   Price ... 1 – 2 – 3 – 4 – 5 – 6 – 7 – 8 – 9 – 10 ... Closing Process

   Why? _____

   _____

8. Salespeople have to understand *assumptive* closing in Step 6 and master a half dozen simple 'Either / Or' non-price 'value' closing questions.

   As a dealership, do we close on price – or do we close on value?

   Price ... 1 – 2 – 3 – 4 – 5 – 6 – 7 – 8 – 9 – 10 ... Value

   Why? _____

   _____

9. In Step 7, salespeople have to master *action closes,* so the customer *makes those mental decisions* that equal, "I'm buying this vehicle now."

   As a dealership, do we close on price – or on taking mental ownership?

   Price ... 1 – 2 – 3 – 4 – 5 – 6 – 7 – 8 – 9 – 10 ... Mental Ownership

   Why? _____

   _____

10. Asking a customer what they 'want' for their trade is suicide before you start working the deal because their figure will almost always be unrealistic. The 'silent walk around' of the trade is to bring the customer's *hope to get* numbers back to reality, without the salesperson saying a word.

As a dealership, do we ask them what they want – or follow this process?

We Ask ... 1 – 2 – 3 – 4 – 5 – 6 – 7 – 8 – 9 – 10 ... Silent Walk Around

Why? _____

_____

11. Salespeople need to know gas mileage, annual miles driven, and any maintenance expenses on the trade, so they can use the *gas savings* and *maintenance* closes in the negotiation to help solve any budget concerns customers have.

As a dealership, do we drop price in the negotiation – or use these closes?

Drop Price ... 1 – 2 – 3 – 4 – 5 – 6 – 7 – 8 – 9 – 10 ... Use These Closes

Why? _____

_____

12. To set up an effective negotiation (working the deal) a salesperson's final closing question has to be a non-price 'Either / Or' close as they move inside to start the paperwork.

As a dealership, is our final 'go inside' close on price – or on value?

Still On Price ... 1 – 2 – 3 – 4 – 5 – 6 – 7 – 8 – 9 – 10 ... On Value

Why? _____

_____

13. Once inside, salespeople have to use the paperwork correctly to start the negotiation. Has the customer made that, *'I'm inside because I'm buying this right now'* mental commitment, before you start your negotiation?

As a dealership, are we sloppy on paperwork – or using it effectively?

Still On Price ... 1 – 2 – 3 – 4 – 5 – 6 – 7 – 8 – 9 – 10 ... On Value

Why? _____

_____

14. Negotiation is the last, most critical step.

As a dealership, do we wing it – or use Joe's 3-Pass Process?

Wing It ... 1 – 2 – 3 – 4 – 5 – 6 – 7 – 8 – 9 – 10 ... Use A Clear Process

Why? _____

_____

The highest score possible is 140 – our score is _____.
If you want to improve your gross – just improve your score.

Why So Much Focus On 'Price'?

Almost everyone in the car business – dealers, managers & salespeople, has a career habit of focusing on price in almost every aspect of the sale. There is also a non-stop 'marketing noise' in our industry about price that's almost impossible to ignore.

There's ... full price disclosure, price transparency, aggressive pricing, value pricing and one price strategies. And then there are reports every day about how every buyer group from 'Gen Z Boomlets' just headed to high school to the Ys, Xs, Boomers, Matures and GI generation, is carefully selecting the exact vehicle they'll buy & that each group is totally price focused.

Dealers also spend thousands of dollars per month on inventory management software *marketed as a value pricing tool.* Using it costs them millions in revenue every year because they're selling cars they would have sold anyway, but at lower gross PVR. Value pricing logic assumes 'every' buyer has seen 'every' vehicle in your market, and has gotten comparison pricing on all of them, and that's never true, and everyone reading this knows it.

Stop, and separate 'marketing' from what really happens on the lot.

Selection ...

- Marketing: 90+% have been online and selected a vehicle to buy.
- On the lot: 86% don't buy what they planned to buy. They did their research, but *their final decision happens on the lot*, not on the internet.

Pricing ...

- Marketing: Everything is about price and if you aren't lowest, you lose.
- Survey: Price didn't even make the top 10 and it's #16 on the vehicle itself.
- On the lot: You can't point to 5 deals you worked last week that didn't pay you more for the vehicle, who didn't take less for their trade, or who didn't make a higher payment than they said they would.

Price is important, but it is almost never 'most' important.

When you really look at 90% of the sales you make, the deal breaker is budget (down and payments), not price. That fact alone means you should never bring price (or trade value) into the conversation on the lot, because it changes the focus and confuses the issue.

Seriously ... when your salespeople learn to handle price correctly, most of the other problems that come up during the sale disappear.

Call now and either get to our sales workshop or take the "PRICE" course on JVTN® so you understand pricing from the customer's side, and learn how to deal with it in every situation that comes up during the sale.

Common Response On Improving Gross

"But Joe, we get all we can – we cannot raise the gross!"

A lot of people really believe it's impossible to raise the gross and I understand because that's how I felt for years when I struggled with price. Then I learned two things – one, I could increase the gross *by improving my skills,* and two, I could continue to raise it *some,* as long as I kept improving.

Easy question ... Can you increase the gross just $5 per unit?

Seriously, on your next deal, could you bump it $5? I'm not talking about a monthly payment that's $5 higher, I'm just talking about charging a total of $5 more than you'd normally take for the vehicle.

"Yeah sure, but Joe – $5 bucks doesn't really matter or prove you can hold more gross." Actually, it does both.

$5 x 100 units is $500 more per month / $6,000 more per year and $3,600 more in net profit per year. Small, yes – worth it? Absolutely!

> *Just by getting $5 more on every deal raises*
> *the gross $6,000 and bumps net profit by .72%.*

Here's another question: If you can raise gross *anytime* by $5, and if your average gross is $1,700 now and you increase it by $5 to get it to $1,705, wouldn't it be true that at that point, you could raise it $5 again? (Say 'yes'.)

The math is scary on these improvements. Raise your average gross **$5 every week**, and in a year it's up $260 per unit. ($5 x 52 weeks = $260.)

That extra $260 PVR generates an extra $187,200 in net per year.

Just crack open the 'door of opportunity' on gross and the sky is the limit.

Try this – when you think your next deal is 'there', tell the salesperson to stick out their hand to shake and say, "My manager said you wouldn't let $10 bucks stand in the way of getting your new car, was he right?" At least half will pay, so you just raised your average gross by $5. Go ahead, try it – it's fun.

Once they get good, switch the question to payments, "My manager said you wouldn't let $10 a month stand in the way, was he right...?" You'll get half to agree, and $5 x 60 months is $300 / $250 in gross. Holy smokes, that's another $180,000 in additional net profit every year.

Give gross a chance – you'll love it!

What's Our Potential To Raise The Gross?

The Potential You See In Your Dealership

1. ✍ List every salesperson in the first line, then in the '+ $_____ per unit' blank, write in how much you feel that person can realistically improve *their gross per unit* if they knew more or just worked the deal better.

Salesperson	Improvement	Salesperson	Improvement
_____	+ $_____ per unit	_____	+ $_____ per unit
_____	+ $_____ per unit	_____	+ $_____ per unit
_____	+ $_____ per unit	_____	+ $_____ per unit
_____	+ $_____ per unit	_____	+ $_____ per unit
_____	+ $_____ per unit	_____	+ $_____ per unit
_____	+ $_____ per unit	_____	+ $_____ per unit
_____	+ $_____ per unit	_____	+ $_____ per unit
_____	+ $_____ per unit	_____	+ $_____ per unit

Total improvement from all of your salespeople... $ _____ Per Unit

2. ✍ **The Math:** If they had more effective selling skills, could bypass price and build value, and had more confidence working deals...

a. In #1, we could realistically increase gross by $_____ per unit

b. We currently deliver _____ units per mo.

c. 'a' x 'b' would add *good gross* of $ _____,_____ per month

d. At 60% of 'c' to net, we'd *net an extra* $ _____,_____ per month

e. In one year, that extra net profit would be $___ , _____ , _____

3. ✍ **WIIFM** (What's In It For Me?) If we did a better job of selling and delivered those extra units every month...

I'd personally earn an extra $ _____ per month,

and that means I'd make $ _____ more per year.

The key to selling: Prove the 'value' that the customer wants.

RAISE THE GROSS

My Action Page & 90 Day Goal

1. *Remember...*

Buying Is Not About Price

Buying Is Not About Price

Buying Is Not About Price

2. Did you circle the 'Skills That Affect Gross' that you know you can quickly improve, at least some?

3. ✍ My 90 day goal: We will improve our gross per unit by $ _____, by ___ / ___ / ___. (Start small if you need to, it all adds up.)

4. ✍ The steps we'll take to reach our goal on raising the gross are...

    1. _____

    2. _____

    3. _____

    4. _____

    5. _____

    ✓ Tip: Give each manager a small group of salespeople to train, coach and manage to help each salesperson achieve their individual goals.

    ✓ Tip: Take my 'PRICE' course on JVTN® and I guarantee if your salespeople and managers apply what we cover, gross will improve.

5. Keep the focus on gross *every day.* Hold a short management meeting each morning *just* on your goal and progress on raising the gross until you've reached your goal. Once you do, stabilize your processes, and then set your next level goal for improvement and get to work.

A Good Deal is a 'Feeling', not a 'Number'.

Grinding out deals is so 'Old School'. It wasn't the right way to hold gross and build your business 30 years ago, and it definitely isn't the way to do it now.

Notice that none of these comments like the one below, talk about tricking anybody, or pushing them into buying something they don't want.

Every comment says just the opposite, "Now I slow down, treat everybody as a buyer, do a better job and my customers love me."

Sure, people want a good deal. Help them find the right car, work the deal for shorter terms with more down to lower their payments, and save them money in interest – and they'll trade their car back in to you sooner.

"From $29,000 ➤ $116,000 ➤ $140,000 per year!"

"I've been in the car business for 5 years. We started on JVTN® 3 years ago, and I have been dedicated to it from the beginning.

Some of the things I've learned are to **stop pre-qualifying**, to **slow things down** and to just **treat everyone like a buyer**. I learned how to **handle objections** and to never give up, whether I'm **closing** or **following up** with my customers.

My results have been incredible and in just 3 years, I've gone from making $29,000 per year to $116,000 last year, and I am on track for $140,000 this year.

JVTN® is the most incredible tool for training, and your training is like magic – it's the perfect process for success!"

– Dustin Rudolph, Salesperson
Metro Mitsubishi, Dartmouth, Nova Scotia

Those are huge results for Dustin and his dealership!

If Dustin's pay went up $111,000 – his dealership's gross went up 3 to 5 times that. Best of all, because it's 'good gross', 60% of that total gross becomes bottom line profit (around $200,000 to $300,000) from just one salesperson.

✍ Write Out Your Thoughts On When & Where
Your Managers And Salespeople Focus On Price
And How That Costs You Sales & Gross

_____

_____

_____

_____

_____

_____

_____

_____

_____

_____

_____

_____

_____

_____

_____

_____

_____

_____

_____

_____

_____

_____

If you're reading this, highlighting key points, filling in the blanks and taking notes, you are not one of the dealers or managers who were just sitting on a Gold Mine anymore. Congratulations, you're digging!

CheckList

Generating More Sales & Good Gross
From The Floor Traffic We Have Now

So far, you're improving sales and good gross...

1) by getting more prospects behind the wheel,
2) by improving your salespeople's skills, and
3) you're improving the gross by focusing more on what the customer wants and needs and less on price.

☑ Salespeople: We're Improving The Number Of Demos

☑ Salespeople: We're Improving Selling Skills & Processes

☑ Salespeople: We're Focusing Less On Price – And More On Value

Now let's look at the final step in dealing with customers on the lot – Desking & Negotiating (working deals), and let's identify your opportunities for management to improve sales, profits (and customer satisfaction) even more.

Next...

❏ Management: Working Every Deal To Negotiate For More Sales & Maximum Gross

FLOOR TRAFFIC
SOLUTION #4

WORKING DEALS
DELIVER MORE UNITS AND
MAXIMIZE THE GROSS

When we talk about gross profit in our 2-Day Desking & Negotiation Workshops, we always start by telling everyone *not to answer out loud*, but just think about this question...

**"Which manager in your dealership
has the lowest gross when they work a deal?"**

Well that never works, because there are usually several managers together in class from each dealership, and people just can't stop themselves from responding *immediately*.

Every time, the manager with the worst gross gets that sheepish grin on his face and lowers his head while all of the other managers from that dealership turn to look at him/her.

We keep it fun, but this is huge when it comes to making or missing more net profit every year, and I'll show you why.

WORKING DEALS FOR
MORE SALES & MAXIMUM GROSS

Just Read The Next 4 Pages & Add An Extra Month
Of Good Gross Profit Every Year

How much lower is the gross when the lowest gross managers
work a deal – and why do some managers have low gross on their deals?

That's easy, some are better at working deals than others.

Of course some managers are better at working deals and holding gross than others. But why? I don't know your managers or why, but you do.

✍ Check the likely causes in your dealership for lower gross deals worked...

❑ we have the wrong person to begin with,

❑ we don't really have a desking process,

❑ we have a process, but that person won't follow it,

❑ we let each manager work deals however they want to,

❑ maybe they think price is most important, or

❑ maybe it's from the desking & negotiation skills they don't have (yet),

❑ or it could be fear and a lack of confidence in working deals for gross,

❑ or it could be that they're too easy and let the salespeople work them harder than they work the customer on each deal,

❑ or they're desperate or more afraid of losing a deal than making $$$,

❑ or they're afraid to say 'no',

❑ or they let salespeople work deals that aren't committed to buy,

❑ or it could just be a bad habit they've developed,

❑ or maybe it's because no one expects them to improve,

– or _____

– or _____

Whatever the reasons, it costs you money every month.

Do the math on what even one low gross manager who works deals costs you each year. Here's a hint in that 100 unit dealership:

The lowest grossing manager may cost you as much as...

One full month
of gross profit every year.

HOW TO REALISTICALLY IMPROVE
THE NET PROFIT $119,988

Same 100 unit dealership ... $700 in F&I & $1,800 up front.

That means the <u>total monthly front end</u> gross is $180,000.

First, track the deals each manager works to find everyone's average, then print the report or chart and start improving that person's gross (and everyone else's, too).

Let's keep it simple and for this example, let's assume there are 3 managers and that they all work the same number of deals (33.33) – and the lowest gross manager is $500 lower than the other two.

Yes, finance gross would improve, too, but let's just focus on what lower front end gross costs you every year.

Increase Your Net With A Better Desking Process

How much more gross profit would you make every year by improving that lowest manager's gross by just $500?

– $500	**Lower gross per unit**	
x 33.33	Deals worked each month	
– $16,665	In lost *front end* gross per month	
– $199,980	**In lost *front end* gross every year**	
x 60%	That would be good gross to net	
$119,988	**Additional Net Profit Per Year**	

Your Added Cost ... $2,390

Train that manager to work deals more effectively in our 2 workshops on Closing and Negotiating, so you can pick up an **extra $119,988 in net profit** each year.

Just get that manager to our 2 workshops...

1. "Closing & Negotiating" for all salespeople and managers
2. "Desking & Negotiating" just for managers

Why both? Because managers have to know exactly how the vehicle is being sold so they can keep their deals on budget, too, instead of price.

DESKING & NEGOTIATION POTENTIAL

What's The Potential You See In Your Dealership?

1. ✏ Pull up your gross and units by the manager who worked the deal. Just print the report from your system and you'll see who can improve.

   As you look at reports like these, it's important to always use a 90 day average on any area you want to improve. Why 90 days? Because months fluctuate – while 3 month rolling averages are your trend. We call your 90 day average, your 'current average' in that category because anything past the last 3 months is really just 'history', and is no longer current.

   From your report, list the managers who work deals and their *current averages* for front end gross, F&I gross, deals they work and deals they deliver. Then write in your realistic potential if *all managers* improve, at least some.

Manager On Deal	Avg. Front	Avg. F&I	Avg. Total	Avg. # Worked	Avg. # Delivered
_____	$ _____	$ _____	$ _____	_____	_____
_____	$ _____	$ _____	$ _____	_____	_____
_____	$ _____	$ _____	$ _____	_____	_____
_____	$ _____	$ _____	$ _____	_____	_____

2. ✏ **The Math:** Seeing the averages by manager in each category, I think if **all** of our managers focused on improving their Desking & Neg. skills...

   a. We could realistically increase gross by $ _____ **per deal**

   b. Our current average number of deals is   _____ units / mo.

   c. 'a' x 'b' would add *good gross* of $ _____,_____ per month

   d. At 60% of 'c' to net, we'd *net an extra* $ _____,_____ per month

   e. In one year, that extra net profit would be $___ , _____ , _____

   * The math in #2 doesn't include gross from the extra units they'd sell by improving. When you factor in that, the improvements are huge and could take the lowest gross manager to becoming the top overall grossing manager.

3. ✏ **WIIFM** (What's In It For Me?) If we did a better job of desking and focused more on budget in our negotiations....

   I'd personally earn an extra $ _____ per month,

   and that means I'd make $ _____ more per year.

NEGOTIATION & DESKING

My Action Page & 90 Day Goal

1. Some managers make working deals look easy and some can't do it because they need just need a little more training.

   In our Desking & Negotiating Workshop, we teach a very simple 3-pass process that every salesperson and manager can master. It's effective and repeatable on every deal, it's customer friendly, easy to follow, and will help you maximize the gross and deliver more units.

   Whether you use our process after class or create your own, you need three things to improve sales and gross at the desk...

   • **Processes** ... You need a clear, effective and repeatable selling process every salesperson follows, and then a clear, effective and repeatable desking process (working the deal) every manager follows and tracks.

   • **Skills** ... Your salespeople's skills at building value and getting 'non-price' buying commitments (closing) – and your manager's skills at working the deal and controlling the process, determine whether the next deal you see becomes a delivery or just another write up you couldn't put together.

   • **Consistency** ... Work every deal the same way every time, and you'll increase sales and gross profit on the vehicle and in F&I, and you'll improve customer satisfaction. Yes, the customers are different, but the steps of a successful negotiation process are always the same.

2. ✍ My 90 day goal: We will improve our average gross to $ _____ by working deals more effectively. Tip: Use our calculators at JoeVerde.com/calc7

3. ✍ The steps we'll take to reach our goal on improving our processes, our skills and our managers who work deals, are...

   1. _____
      _____

   2. _____
      _____

   3. _____
      _____

   ✓ Tip: Create a 'goals' book for yourself. A simple spiral notebook or 3 ring binder works great.

   ✓ Tip: See the information at the back of this book about our sales, closing, and negotiation workshops and get everyone trained right this year. You'll be glad you did.

4. Hold a short management meeting each morning to go over everyone's averages on the deals they've worked.

So Far We've Found An Extra

$2,405,988

In 'Zero Expense' Net Profit
Just From Existing Floor Traffic

We just covered *four 'no expense' ways* a 100 unit dealership can **realistically increase net profit from $500,000 to $2,905,988 per year** at zero expense with the floor traffic they already have now!

4 ways to increase your net profit with just your floor traffic...

  1. Improve Selling Skills & Processes

  2. Demonstrate Vehicles To More Customers

  3. Talk Price Less To Increase Gross Profit

  4. Improve Desking & Negotiation Skills

Net Profit Potential
From The Floor Traffic You Have Now

$500,000 Current Net Profit

+ $2,405,988 Extra

$2,905,988

✍ Which of your salespeople and managers
need to improve in each of these areas we've covered?

1. Which salespeople and managers need to improve their **core selling skills** throughout the selling, closing and negotiation process?

   _____   _____   _____
   _____   _____   _____
   _____   _____   _____

2. Which salespeople need to improve their **demo** percentages and quality?

   _____   _____   _____
   _____   _____   _____

3. Which managers need to do better at **expecting and requiring** salespeople to do more and better demos to improve unit sales and gross profit?

   _____   _____   _____
   _____   _____   _____

4. Which salespeople and managers need to change their focus throughout the selling, closing and negotiation process **to building more value** in our dealership and our products, instead of focusing every deal on price?

   _____   _____   _____
   _____   _____   _____
   _____   _____   _____

5. Can our **desking and negotiation** process be improved? ❑ Yes ❑ No

6. Which salespeople and managers need to improve their **skills at working deals** (the negotiation and desking processes)?

   _____   _____   _____
   _____   _____   _____
   _____   _____   _____

7. To make all of the needed improvements above – which managers will need to improve their **core management skills**; daily training, daily coaching, and daily management of our selling processes & activities?

   _____   _____   _____
   _____   _____   _____

Change for growth in business starts from the top down.
Growth never starts from the bottom up.

"I increased my commissions $400 per unit and my customers like me even more!"

"I train on JVTN® and I also recently attended your Closing & Negotiating Workshop and WOW! The information and energy I picked up from the workshop truly increased my confidence and enthusiasm for this business.

After learning the **3-pass budget focused negotiation** process, I almost felt it was too easy to go back and ask for all of the money. So I did, and it worked!

I increased my commission per unit by $400 and made more money than ever, and had **more customers that liked me** even more!

By focusing on the **value** and getting **more $ down**, I was able to get **more deals financed**, and was able to deliver more vehicles on **shorter terms**…which means I would have that customer back that much faster for their next vehicle.

Thanks Joe, for giving us back the secret to having more fun and making more money!"

– Omar Vasconez, Salesperson
Ed Bozarth Chevrolet Buick, Grand Junction, Colorado

✍ Let's do the math on Omar's improvement…

If Omar picked up an extra $400 per unit by **closing on budget** in the negotiation, that's $1,500 to $1,600 per unit for the dealership.

If he's selling 15 units, that's another $20,000–$24,000 in good gross every month – for about $150,000 more net profit per year.

Plus, his customers are happier because he's made their buying experience with him and his dealership **about value, not price.** And they're even happier because his negotiations are focused on helping them fit it into their budget instead of becoming that long, drawn out back and forth price grind people hate.

Focusing on 'Value' and 'Budget'
totally changes the Negotiation process.

Congratulations Brandon!

"Half a million dollars *more* per month..."

*"From 130 units at $2,700 per unit
to 239 units at $4,100 per unit with Joe's training."*

"I started in sales at a Dodge store with no experience in the car business, and went to Joe Verde training before I did anything else.

My third month, I became salesman of the month and then salesman of the year. My dealership was the #1 in the nation and I pride myself on being the #1 salesperson at the #1 dealership.

I moved to Texas to be closer to family and went to work at the Dodge dealership. I was salesman of the month my first 2 months and they'd never seen anything like the Joe Verde processes.

They didn't know the steps to the sale, they didn't know how to stay off price or how to sell the car. So they promoted me to manager and at 25, I was the youngest manager the store ever had.

I hold training Monday through Friday from 10:15 to 11:15 every morning. We cover Joe's steps, or closes or whatever else we need to focus on that day.

When I started training, the store was doing 130 units per month at $2,700 per copy. Last month we did 239 at about $4,100 each.

*That's 100 more units and way over
a half a million dollar improvement in gross every month.*

The guys have improved, the store has improved and it's from Joe Verde training every single day!

Thank you Joe, I attribute everything to your training and I am your biggest advocate."

*– Brandon Bourke
General Sales Manager, Dodge, Texas*

Results

"From 5 to 19.5 units a month!"

"Joe, my story begins when I lost my business and got into the car business...

I tried it my way with **no training and I sold 5 cars.**

Then, I **started training on JVTN®** and watched a chapter on the greeting, practiced it and it worked!

I continued taking courses believing that if I implemented what I was learning, it would make a difference, and it did.

Thanks to your training, I went from **10 the next month** to **18.5** and then to **19.5** and then to leading the board and **earning over $100,000 in less than a year!**

And I went from living in an apartment with my wife and 4 kids to a beautiful home, a new car and all the other things that matter.

More importantly, your training gave me the **confidence** to know that I have found the career I want to be in.

I'm a Manager now and I get to teach other people the impact your training will have in their own lives."

– Nathan Syme, Sales Manager
Ed Bozarth Chevrolet, Las Vegas, Nevada

Results

"From 4-6 units to my first $10,000 month."

"I started at Sierra Blanca about a year ago. My first few months I was at 4-6 units. After consistently **training on JVTN®**, my average went to 10-12 units. Then the light bulb really came on after attending your sales workshop.

When I came back, I increased my average to 12-15 and this month I'm just shy of **a $10,000 month** and the day isn't over!

By mastering my questions and learning to properly help the customer, I am on my way to being a 20+ car professional."

– Jared Storey, Salesperson
Sierra Blanca Motors, Ruidoso, New Mexico

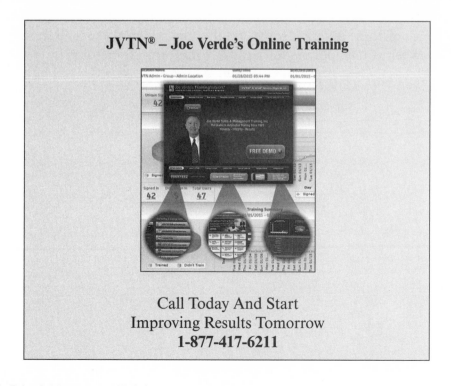

JVTN® – Joe Verde's Online Training

Call Today And Start
Improving Results Tomorrow
1-877-417-6211

QUICK TIP

You must have a ton of great ideas by now!

Here's a quick tip I use to save time in the future...

I take a lot of notes on dozens of topics and keep them in a tabbed, 3-ring binder. Then depending on the importance of that note or idea, I transfer them to a Word® document in my computer, or to the 'Notes' app in my iPhone.

That way, whether they're in the binder or the document, I can keep them sorted by 'subject' and when I get another idea on that topic, I can easily add more notes at any time.

If you'll do the same, you can refer back to your ideas on all of these different topics on the spot, or even years later when you're looking for a quick solution to something.

*You'll be surprised how often you've already
solved a problem and have just forgotten.*

UNSOLD BUYER FOLLOW UP

SOLUTION #5

Who are your hottest prospects?

Other than the people on the lot right now, *your hottest prospect just left without buying.*

Four Benefits Of Unsold Follow Up

You've already gone to the expense to put this customer on the lot the first time, so when you bring more unsold customers back into your dealership through training and by implementing an effective unsold follow up process, you'll...

1. Sell more units at no extra expense

2. Increase your "Good Gross" profit

3. Lower your overall cost per sale

4. Increase your net profit

Remember, 8 out of 10 people were buyers when they first came onto the lot. That also means 8 out of 10 people who leave are still buyers – and they will be buying from someone, very soon.

WHICH OF THESE FACTS
AFFECT YOUR PAYCHECK?

✍ *Circle the # for each fact that affects your paycheck and fill in the blanks...*

1. **8 out of 10 ... 80% were buyers when they came on to your lot, and that means 80% of the people who leave without buying are still buyers and will either buy from you or a competitor.**

   ✍ How does this fact affect our sales and gross profit potential?_____
   _____

   ✍ What are we not doing that costs us sales and profit? _____
   _____
   _____

   ✍ Which of our salespeople & managers need to buy into this fact, so we can sell more units each month?

   _____   _____   _____   _____   _____   _____   _____
   _____   _____   _____   _____   _____   _____   _____

   ✍ How much does this cost me personally each month? $_____

2. **9 out of 10 ... 90% of the people who leave without buying are not asked for their contact information by the salesperson – who's going to need this information if they're going to follow up.**

   ✍ How does this fact affect our sales and gross profit potential?_____
   _____

   ✍ Do we have a clear process, and is it being followed? ❑ Yes ❑ No
   _____

   ✍ Which of our salespeople need to get contact info more often?

   _____   _____   _____   _____   _____   _____   _____

   ✍ How much does this cost me personally each month? $_____

3. **9 out of 10 ... 90% of those unsold customers are never contacted again about buying after they leave the dealership.**

   ✍ How does this fact affect our sales and gross profit potential?_____
   _____

   ✍ Who is teaching and requiring our salespeople to get contact info?
   _____
   _____

   ✍ Which salespeople need to contact more of their unsold customers?

   _____   _____   _____   _____   _____   _____   _____

   ✍ How much does this cost me personally each month? $_____

4. **Minutes matter ...** People only stop at 2 dealerships before they purchase, so the longer you take to make that first follow up contact after they leave, the less likely you are to see them again.

    Within 3-5 minutes of the customer leaving, your salesperson should make their 1st contact with a compelling reason to come back in right away.

    ✍ How does this fact affect our sales and gross profit potential?_____

    _____

    ✍ Do we have a clear process, and is it being followed? ❑ Yes ❑ No

    _____

    ✍ Which of our salespeople need to follow up sooner than they are now?

    _____ _____ _____ _____ _____ _____ _____

    ✍ How much does this cost me personally each month? $_____

5. **3 out of 9 ... With effective follow up, 33% (1/3) of the people who leave without buying will come back to your dealership.**

    ✍ How does this fact affect our sales and gross profit potential?_____

    _____

    ✍ How many be-backs would this mean for our dealership?

    _____

    ✍ Which of our salespeople & managers need to understand the impact this fact can have on our sales volume and gross profit?

    _____ _____ _____ _____ _____ _____ _____

    _____ _____ _____ _____ _____ _____ _____

    ✍ How much does this cost me personally each month? $_____

6. **2 out of 3 ... 67% of the people who do come back into the dealership, buy the vehicle on the spot. That's a 67% closing ratio on be-backs.**

    ✍ How does this fact affect our sales and gross profit potential?_____

    _____

    ✍ How many additional sales would this mean for our dealership?

    _____

    ✍ Which of our salespeople & managers need to understand the impact this fact can have on our sales volume and gross profit?

    _____ _____ _____ _____ _____ _____ _____

    _____ _____ _____ _____ _____ _____ _____

    ✍ How much does this cost me personally each month? $_____

7. **Almost Zero Competition ...** 90% of your competition isn't trained to get contact information and isn't trained or required to follow up. That means you and your salespeople have almost zero competition for this customer.

✍ How does this fact affect our sales and gross profit potential?_____
_____
_____

✍ With practically no competition for these unsold customers, what training, processes and accountability do we need now to get more of these easy sales we're losing each month? _____
_____
_____

✍ Are managers and salespeople trained properly? ❏ Yes ❏ No
If not, why not? _____
_____

✍ Do we have clear, effective processes? ❏ Yes ❏ No
If not, why not? _____
_____

✍ Are management & sales held accountable? ❏ Yes ❏ No
If not, why not? _____
_____

If you checked 'no' to the last 3 questions, you're missing out on a realistic potential 67% increase in your sales and gross profit.

✍ Which of our salespeople and managers need to improve, so we can improve sales & gross for the dealership...

_____ _____ _____ _____ _____ _____ _____

_____ _____ _____ _____ _____ _____ _____

✍ How much does this cost me personally each month? $_____

**Do The Math – Training Your Salespeople
To Follow Up Correctly Saves You Thousands**

There just aren't many lookers or shoppers anymore. People do their research and only stop at a couple of dealerships before they buy.

You can quickly train your salespeople on JVTN® to follow up and get customers back on the lot and enjoy a 67% closing ratio – **or** – you can spend $100-$500 more in advertising *per person* to put another customer on the lot with just a 20% chance of making that sale.

If you're on JVTN®, take our 15 chapter course,
"Turn Unsold Customers Into Be-Backs & Deliveries"

How To Realistically Improve Sales 67% & Triple Your Net

Expense So Far: $300-$500 Per Prospect

Return So Far On This Unsold Prospect: $0

Here again, dealers don't need more leads to sell more units. In fact, this lead is bought, paid for and didn't buy. Now there's a chance to recoup your investment and earn more 'Good Gross'.

Here's the math again in that 100 unit dealership...

500	People are on the lot each month
400	Didn't buy, but now after training, SP get...
x 75%	Contact info on everyone who left
300	**Left – but _now_ SP get their contact information**
x 33%	Will come back in with good follow up
100	People come back in (be-backs)
x 67%	Will buy on their second visit
67	**Sales from your effective unsold follow up**
x $2,500	Average gross per unit
$167,500	Additional Good Gross each month
x 60%	Good Gross to Net Profit
$100,500	**Additional Net Profit per month**

Triple Your Net With Unsold Follow Up

$1,206,000

Additional **Net Profit** per year

Your Cost To Increase Sales & Net Profit ... $1,270

*If you're on JVTN® take the course on how to follow up
every unsold prospect and then just follow my 6 steps every time.*

UnSold Follow Up Potential
What's The Potential You See In Your Dealership?

1. ✍ List the salespeople who could sell more units each month by improving their unsold follow up skills.

    What is a realistic improvement of the <u>additional units</u> each person could sell with more effective unsold follow up skills and a clear process?

Salesperson	Improvement	Salesperson	Improvement
_____	by + ___units	_____	by + ___units
_____	by + ___units	_____	by + ___units
_____	by + ___units	_____	by + ___units
_____	by + ___units	_____	by + ___units
_____	by + ___units	_____	by + ___units
_____	by + ___units	_____	by + ___units
_____	by + ___units	_____	by + ___units

Total improvement from all of your salespeople...   **+ _____ Units**

2. ✍ **The Math:** If we improved each salesperson's *selling skills* and had a clear step-by-step unsold follow up process in our dealership that we managed more effectively each day...

    a. We could realistically sell ____ **more units per mo.**

    b. Using our total sales and F&I gross of $ _____ per unit

    c. 'a' x 'b' would add *good gross* of $ _____,_____ per month

    d. At 60% of 'c' to net, we'd *net an extra* $ _____,_____ per month

    e. In one year, that extra net profit would be $ ___ , _____ , _____

3. ✍ **WIIFM** (What's In It For Me?) If we taught our salespeople how to sell, and did a better job handling our 'unsold' prospects and delivered those extra units every month...

    I'd personally earn an extra $ _____ per month,

    and that means I'd make $ _____ more per year.

UNSOLD FOLLOW UP
My Action Page & 90 Day Goal

1. Easy steps to sell more of your unsold prospects...

   • Track (count) every person who shows any interest at all in a vehicle. That includes lookers, service customers, kids, etc.

   • Find *your dealership's* stats: Traffic, demos, write ups, sales, contact info on unsold – contact attempts, appointments, shows, deliveries & gross.

   • Teach your salespeople how to get contact information on everyone.

   • Start each day with a list of everyone who didn't buy and contact them.

   • Except when they've tried and really can't get them back in, don't make your salespeople's calls for them.

   The goal is to teach them how to do this for themselves. So sit with them regularly as they make their calls. It's easy...

   1) Sell them on the benefit.
   2) Teach them how.
   3) Make a call or two for them to show them how easy it is.
   4) Listen to their first few calls and help them improve.

   "Tell me and I forget, teach me and I may remember, involve me and I learn." – Ben Franklin

2. ✐ My 90 day goal: We will improve our unsold follow up contact percentages from _____ % now to _____ % by ___ / ___ / ___.

3. ✐ The steps we'll take to reach our goals on unsold follow up are...

   1. _____
   _____

   2. _____
   _____

   3. _____
   _____

   ✓ Tip: Give each manager a small group of salespeople to train, coach and manage to help each salesperson achieve their individual goals.

4. Keep the focus on unsold follow up *every day.* Hold a short management meeting each morning *just* on your goal and progress to improve your unsold follow up, until you've reached your goal.

**"I went from 8 to 15 units.
My new goal is 20."**

"I have been in the car business 7 months. I started out with an 8-car month, thought I was great, got a little cocky, dropped to 3.

We got JVTN® online training at the dealership and using it helped me understand the **step-by-step process of selling cars** and now I'm averaging 15 units.

The 2-Day Sales Workshop I just attended really put everything into perspective, and my new goal is to raise my average to 20.

Everyone should attend this class because you really can sell more if you just **follow the basic steps** to the sale."

– Erin Cook, Salesperson
Birchwood Infiniti Nissan, Winnipeg, Manitoba

✍ Write Out Your Thoughts On The Potential
You See With Unsold Follow Up In Your Dealership

_____

_____

_____

_____

_____

_____

_____

_____

_____

_____

_____

_____

_____

_____

_____

_____

_____

_____

_____

_____

_____

_____

_____

_____

_____

_____

_____

Go back and highlight your 3 most important ideas on unsold follow up.

In your 3-ring binder, add a blank page for each of the 3 key points on unsold follow up and start making notes. Then just like we're doing here, list who could improve and how, and create an action plan.

When you really focus on improving your people, your sales and your gross, instead of always trying to buy more sales, this really is fun and profitable.

Quiz

What 3 things do you need for Unsold Customer Follow Up, Incoming Sales Calls, and most Internet Leads to turn each of those contacts into an appointment that will show?

A Phone + Selling Skills + A Process

INCOMING SALES CALLS

SOLUTION #6

Improve Your Salespeople's
Selling Skills & Your Processes
And Deliver More Units

You don't need more floor traffic to sell more units, and you don't need more incoming calls or internet leads either. Your salespeople just need better selling skills, and a step-by-step process they're required to follow to turn your incoming calls and leads into deliveries and more net profit.

It's easy to get these two confused...
Getting *more* leads doesn't equal *better* results.
Getting *better* at handling leads equals *more* results.

WHICH OF THESE FACTS
AFFECT YOUR PAYCHECK?

✍ *Circle the # for each fact that affects your paycheck and fill in the blanks...*

1. 9 out of 10 ... 90% of incoming callers buy a vehicle within a week.

✍ How does this fact affect our sales and gross profit potential?_____

_____

_____

✍ Which of our salespeople and managers do not understand the volume and profit potential this fact offers on incoming sales calls?

_____ _____ _____ _____ _____ _____ _____

_____ _____ _____ _____ _____ _____ _____

2. Oops ... a few errors stop most prospects from becoming deliveries.

No answer! .... 3 out of 10 calls never make it to the right person.

"Your name?" .... 75% of callers aren't asked for their name.

"Your number?" .... 85% are not asked for their phone number.

"Name & #?" .... 93% are not even asked for basic contact information; their name and their phone number.

"My name is" .... On 92% of calls, salespeople don't even give the caller their own name, in case they do come in.

Set An Appointment ... 97% of the time, salespeople do not schedule a *firm* appointment with the call or lead.

✍ How do these facts affect our sales and gross profit potential? _____

_____

✍ Where and how are we dropping the ball on training and managing our incoming calls and internet leads? _____

_____

_____

_____

✍ Which of our salespeople and managers need to improve in this area, so we can improve sales and gross from our calls and leads...

_____ _____ _____ _____ _____ _____ _____

_____ _____ _____ _____ _____ _____ _____

✍ How much does this cost me personally each month? $_____

3. **No name, no number, no appointment – no surprise...**

88% of incoming callers do not come into the dealership (if they do, it's hard to trace a sale to the incoming call unless the system matches incoming calls and numbers given during the sale).

✎ How does this fact affect our sales and gross profit potential?_____

_____

_____

_____

✎ Which of our salespeople and our managers need to improve so we can improve sales & gross from these calls and leads?

_____ _____ _____ _____ _____ _____ _____

_____ _____ _____ _____ _____ _____ _____

✎ How much does this cost me personally each month? $ _____

4. **'Average' stats when incoming calls are handled correctly...**

- Setting 60% appointments is average
    → ✎ My estimate of our dealership's average: _____%

- 60% of appointments that show up is average
    → ✎ My estimate of our dealership's average: _____%

- 50% of appointments that show, buy on average
    → ✎ My estimate of our dealership's average: _____%

✎ How do these averages affect our sales and gross profit potential? ____

_____

_____

_____

✎ Which of our salespeople and managers need to improve their skills and processes, so we can improve sales & gross from our calls and leads?

_____ _____ _____ _____ _____ _____ _____

_____ _____ _____ _____ _____ _____ _____

✎ How much does this cost me personally each month? $ _____

A Critical Point On Phone Skills

Phone skills are <u>not different</u> skills.

One of the biggest problems most managers *think* they have is that, "Our guys just aren't any good on the phone."

When you look at the average number of sales per salesperson, what you'll find almost every time is that most salespeople aren't any good at selling, period – and it's the lack of good selling skills that is the core problem handling incoming calls & internet leads.

Being successful on the phone requires two things: a clear and effective *process* to follow (the 6 steps to turn a call or inbound lead into an appointment that shows) and the good *selling skills* that the salesperson needs, so they can follow the process.

Why? Because ...

- If a salesperson **can't ask the right questions** to control the conversation on the lot – *they can't control the call either.*

- If they **can't bypass price, or rephrase price** on the lot – *they can't handle price properly on the phone, either.*

- If they **can't deal with objections, expand their inventory, build rapport or close the sale** on the lot – *they can't expand inventory, build rapport, and they certainly can't close on a firm appointment that will show on the phone, either.*

There's no rocket science here – just look at any salesperson who sells 20-30-40+ units per month. They're good at the steps to selling and they're good at unsold follow up. They're good at getting referrals and they're good at turning calls and leads into appointments that show – because they can 'sell'.

They have great selling skills and they also have a clear process to follow when they have a phone in their hand.

Teach your salespeople how to 'sell'. By default, you'll improve sales from your incoming calls and internet leads, too.

HOW TO REALISTICALLY INCREASE
SALES 21 UNITS & YOUR NET $378,000

Could You Use A Few More Sales?

Most dealerships don't track incoming sales calls, appointments, shows and deliveries, but that 100 unit dealership gets about 150 *sales calls* each month.

Here's the math on what happens to those incoming calls...

150	Incoming sales calls
x 90%	Will buy within a week
135	Buyers call in each month
− 6	**Sales, which is typical now from incoming sales calls**
129	**Lost sales now from incoming sales calls**

Easy improvement...

27	Total sales using avg. stats (See 'Facts': #4)
= **21**	**Additional** units per month from incoming calls (6 now + 21 additional units = 27 total sales)
x $2,500	Average gross per unit
$52,500	Additional Good Gross profit per month
$630,000	**More in Good Gross profit per year**
x 60%	Good Gross to Net Profit

Almost Double Your Net From Calls & Leads You Get Now

$378,000+
Additional **Net Profit** per year

Your Cost To Increase Sales & Net Profit ... $1,270

More good news... You can easily do this by teaching your salespeople their core selling skills and our Incoming Sales Call Process. That means you don't need to add any new departments – so you save even more.

OUR INCOMING CALL POTENTIAL
What's The Potential You See In Your Dealership?

1. ✍ List the salespeople who could sell more with better selling skills, which *by default* will improve their Incoming Sales Call skills.

   Then write in a realistic improvement of the <u>additional units</u> each person could sell with a step-by-step process and the skills to turn more calls into appointments that show.

Salesperson	Improvement	Salesperson	Improvement
_____	by + ___units	_____	by + ___units
_____	by + ___units	_____	by + ___units
_____	by + ___units	_____	by + ___units
_____	by + ___units	_____	by + ___units
_____	by + ___units	_____	by + ___units
_____	by + ___units	_____	by + ___units
_____	by + ___units	_____	by + ___units
_____	by + ___units	_____	by + ___units

   Total improvement from all your salespeople...   + _____ Units

2. ✍ **The Math:** If we had a clear process and improved their *selling skills* so they could do a better job on incoming calls, from my estimates above...

   a. We could realistically sell   _____ **more units per mo.**

   b. Using our total sales and F&I gross of $ _____ per unit

   c. 'a' x 'b' would add *good gross* of $ _____,_____ per month

   d. At 60% of 'c' to net, we'd *net an extra* $ _____,_____ per month

   e. In one year, that extra net profit would be $ ___ , _____ , _____

3. ✍ **WIIFM** (What's In It For Me?) If we did a better job on calls and leads, and delivered those extra units every month...

   I'd personally earn an extra $ _____ per month,

   and that means I'd make $ _____ more per year.

INCOMING SALES CALL GOALS
My Action Page & 90 Day Goal

1. These are the *processes* salespeople need to follow to turn more incoming calls and leads into appointments that will show, and the related critical *core selling skills* salespeople need to succeed.

   ✍ *Circle the processes and skills you know they need to improve.*

   a. Process: Build Rapport / Investigate / Expand Inventory
      Skills: Ask Open Ended & 'Either / Or' Questions ... Listen

   b. Process: Get Phone Numbers & Names
      Skills: Ask Direct, Open Ended Questions

   c. Process: Create Urgency
      Skills: Master Related Urgency Statements,
                 Ask Tie Down & 'Either / Or' Questions

   d. Process: Handle Price Questions & Objections
      Skills: Answer & Then Ask A Question
                 Bypass Price / Rephrase Price

   e. Process: Handle Common Objections: Trade Value / Distance
      Skills: CRIC / 2-Step / 1-Step / Zero-Step
                 Ask The Right Questions

   f. Process: Control The Call / Conversation
      Skills: Ask 'Either / Or' Questions

   g. Process: Close On A Firm Appointment & Anchor The Appt.
      Skills: Ask 'Either / Or' & Tie Down Questions

   h. Process: Appointment Verification Before They Come In
      Skills: Ask 'Either / Or' Questions ... Create Urgency

Continued on next page... ⟶

✔ *Tip from our top Internet Dealers:* Don't send a dozen emails back and forth – just pick up the phone and call the number on the lead!

When customers ask about a vehicle, they want a quick response. That's why you're getting fewer internet leads and more incoming calls now.

---

2. ✎ List each salesperson and the process or skill they need to improve to turn more incoming calls and internet leads into appointments that show.

Salesperson   Process / Skill (see the previous page, # a - h)

_____   _____

_____   _____

_____   _____

_____   _____

_____   _____

_____   _____

_____   _____

_____   _____

_____   _____

_____   _____

_____   _____

_____   _____

3. ✎ My 90 day goal: We will improve our incoming call and internet lead appointment percentages from _____ % now to _____ % by ___ / ___ / ___.

4. ✎ The steps we'll take to reach our goals are...

    1. _____

          _____

    2. _____

          _____

    3. _____

          _____

   ✓ Tip: Give each manager a small group of salespeople to train, coach and manage to help each salesperson achieve their individual goals.

5. Keep the focus on incoming calls and leads *every day*. Hold a short management meeting each morning *just* on your goal and progress on improving appointments that show until you've reached your goal.

✍ **Write Down Your Ideas**

Take a few minutes again to think about what you've read
and jot down your ideas now, so you don't misplace them later.

✍ *Other important points for me so far are* _____

_____

_____

_____

_____

_____

_____

_____

_____

_____

✍ *I've also realized* _____

_____

_____

_____

_____

_____

_____

✍ *Other than the goals I've set already, I'll also commit to* _____

_____

_____

_____

_____

_____

_____

_____

"Getting ready is the secret of success."

– Henry Ford

About Those Calls & Internet Leads...

"I'm on pace for another best year ever!"

"Hello Joe,

I've been in the car business just under 2 years and have been training on JVTN® since I started.

I run the **internet department**, and as you know, the key to internet leads is **setting appointments** and thanks to you, I've begun to master it.

In my first 8 months, I sold 75 units and made $60,000. By continuing to train on JVTN® and by **slowing things down**, focusing on **getting them excited about me**, the **vehicle** and the **dealership**, I sold 130 units and made $115,000!

My average **gross went up $600 per car** from my first year to my second! My customers love me, I have the best rating on Dealer Rater, and in just the short time so far this year, I am on pace to top it again!

Thanks for the daily **attitude** adjustment and for the **skills, work habits, and choice of customer focus** (repeat & referrals) I'm continually developing to become a true sales professional."

– Paul C., ISC
Bridge City Chrysler, Lethbridge, Alberta

DAILY PROSPECTING

SOLUTION #7

Generate New Business
Through Daily Prospecting

You hired salespeople to do 3 key things...

1. **Sell** the vehicle once they're with a customer.

2. **Retain** the customers they sell long-term, to become service and parts customers, and for future sales.

3. **Develop** their own business through daily prospecting in service, by phone, by mail or email, and also by prospecting in person.

   Note: When we teach prospecting, we only focus on finding *the next buyer in the family.* And we do that just by talking to people who already know us, or who are already customers of the dealership.

With so many great prospects 'in house'...
*There's **never** a need to have your salespeople*
*make **cold calls to strangers** to sell a car.*

WHICH OF THESE FACTS
AFFECT YOUR PAYCHECK?

✍ *Circle the # for each fact that affects your paycheck and fill in the blanks...*

1. **95% of the people either own a vehicle now or will be getting one.**
    ✍ How does this fact affect our sales and gross profit potential?_____
    _____
    _____

    ✍ Describe the opportunity this fact offers to increase sales and profit?
    _____
    _____

    ✍ List your salespeople & managers who do not see the opportunity...

    _____ _____ _____ _____ _____ _____ _____

    _____ _____ _____ _____ _____ _____ _____

2. **71% bought because they liked the salesperson they worked with.**
    ✍ How does this fact affect our sales and gross profit potential?_____
    _____

    ✍ Which of these groups <u>do not</u> already 'like' your dealership?
    ❑ Walk-Ins   ❑ Sold Cust.   ❑ Service Cust.   ❑ People You Know
    ✍ Which of these groups make up 70% of your vehicle sales now?
    ❑ Walk-Ins   ❑ Sold Cust.   ❑ Service Cust.   ❑ People You Know

3. **30% of all people have a family member who'll be buying a vehicle within 90 days. These are very Hot Prospects.**
    Note: 'All' includes all family, friends, neighbors, service & parts customers, previous customers, everyone in the dealership's CRM / DMS, and everyone else in your community. All means ALL.

    ✍ How does this fact affect our sales and gross profit potential?_____
    _____

    ✍ Which opportunity does this fact offer to increase our sales and profit?
    ❑ Limited Opportunity   ❑ Unlimited Opportunity
    ✍ List your salespeople & managers who do not see the unlimited opportunity prospecting offers to sell more units...

    _____ _____ _____ _____ _____ _____ _____

    _____ _____ _____ _____ _____ _____ _____

    ✍ How much does this cost me personally each month? $_____

4. **62% of all people know someone who'll be buying within 90 days.**

✍ How does this fact affect your sales and gross profit potential? _____

_____

_____

✍ List your salespeople & managers who do not see the unlimited opportunity prospecting offers to sell more units...

_____ _____ _____ _____ _____ _____ _____

_____ _____ _____ _____ _____ _____ _____

✍ How much does this cost me personally each month? $_____

5. **63% have no intention of buying their next vehicle from the same salesperson or dealership where they bought their last vehicle. That's no surprise because...**
   - 90% were never contacted about buying another vehicle.
   - 82% can't remember their last salesperson's name a year later.

✍ How does this fact affect our sales and gross profit potential? _____

_____

✍ List your salespeople & managers who do not see the unlimited opportunity prospecting offers to sell more units...

_____ _____ _____ _____ _____ _____ _____

_____ _____ _____ _____ _____ _____ _____

✍ How much does this cost me personally each month? $_____

6. **Deliver 75% – Increase The Gross – Lower Sales Costs PVR.**
   - **Close More ...** The average closing ratio on a repeat customer or prospect a salesperson or manager brings into the dealership is 75%.
   - **Gross More ...** Gross on a repeat customer, referral or the prospect that a salesperson or manager brings into the dealership, is 40% higher than the average gross on any type of walk-in prospect.
   - **Save More ...** Not only do they pay 40% more in good gross, each repeat or referral sale you make saves you $500 or so in expenses, compared to any ad-driven or purchased lead-driven sale you make.

✍ How do these 3 benefits of dealing with repeats, referrals and outside prospects affect your sales and gross profit potential? _____

_____

_____

_____

Continued on next page... ⟶

✍ List your salespeople & managers who do not see the opportunity prospecting offers to sell more units...

_____ _____ _____ _____ _____ _____ _____

_____ _____ _____ _____ _____ _____ _____

✍ How much does this cost me personally each month? $_____

7. **More Great News ... The average family will purchase about 36 vehicles.**

✍ How does this fact affect our sales and gross profit potential?_____
_____
_____

✍ Select the opportunity this fact offers to increase sales and profit?

❑ Limited Opportunity   ❑ Unlimited Opportunity

✍ List your salespeople & managers who do not see the unlimited opportunity prospecting offers to sell more units...

_____ _____ _____ _____ _____ _____ _____

_____ _____ _____ _____ _____ _____ _____

✍ How much does this cost me personally each month? $_____

8. **No Competition** ... The average dealership sells 75%–80% of their vehicles to expensive, ad-driven, price-shopping, tough to close, lower gross prospects – and only 20% to 25% to easy to close, higher grossing repeat customers, referrals and prospects.

✍ What can we do to take advantage of the unlimited opportunities that daily prospecting offers our dealership? _____
_____
_____
_____

Circle Your Best Opportunity For Continuous Growth...

A. Spend 90% of your time and money *every month* to put more *high cost, tough to close (20%) low gross* customers on the lot.

B. Train your salespeople and managers *one time* to follow up and prospect to generate more *low cost / no cost, easy to close (75%), high gross* prospects with practically $0.^{00} expense per unit sold.

Make the common sense choice – you'll be glad you did.

UNLIMITED OPPORTUNITY

**Prospecting isn't just a Gold Nugget
It's a full blown Gold Mine!**

*This is the hardest group to put an improvement number on,
because your potential is only limited by your commitment.*

Prospecting offers so much opportunity for growth that you could literally stop all advertising, put a chain link fence up around your dealership, only sell to repeat customers, their referrals, to current dealership customers in parts and service, and to prospects your salespeople and managers bring into the dealership ... *and you'd double your sales and increase your net by 943%.*

Imagine being *a high expense, ad-driven dealership* with 10 salespeople selling 100 units at $500,000 net, to becoming a *200 unit dealership with 10 salespeople* (plus 2 or 3 sales assistants) who drive their own business by prospecting, *at $5,200,000 net instead?* (Use the calculator at JoeVerde.com/net7)

Imagine the fun, the growth, the profit and the income for everyone that would be generated with 80% of your sales coming from high profit, low cost, easy to close, friendly people – instead of 80% from ad-driven price shoppers.

**How many Hot Prospects are there *each month*
in a 100 unit dealership that's been in business 10 years?**

500	Customers in service every month
x 30%	Have a family member buying within 90 days
150	**Hot Prospects In Service**
12,000	Previous customers in the CRM (10 years x 1,200 yr.)
x 30%	Family member trading in 90 days
3,600	**Hot Prospects In The CRM / DMS**

✍ **How many Hot Prospects do you have
in your dealership every month right now?**

We have _____ Customers in our **service** department every month.

We have _____ Previous customers and others in our **database**.

Total: _____ **Customers we can prospect *in our dealership* each month.**

x 30% Have a family member who will buy within 90 days.

We have _____ **Hot prospects who'll buy within 90 days, if not from us, from a competitor.** (We'd prefer they buy from us.)

PROSPECTING OPPORTUNITY

*Let's look at the results you could expect from some realistic
daily prospecting in that typical 100 unit dealership...*

Average salespeople have almost 6 hours of down time each day. Considering that's a very large unused block of time, I've used a very low, and very realistic number of prospecting contacts (below).

In fact, you could double this number of contacts – at least until the contacts start to create so much new floor traffic that salespeople are actually *working* most of their shift instead of *waiting* for your dealership to supply them with more expensive, price shopping, harder to close, low gross, walk-in customers.

Question: How long does a 5 minute prospecting call take?

Exactly, about 5 minutes. Keep that '5 minutes per call' in mind as you do the math, before you say they don't have enough time to make these contacts.

1. Prospecting Out In Your Service Drive

Being realistic, have each salesperson talk to just 1 customer in service each day and work our 5 referral / prospecting questions into that conversation.

250	Contacts per mo. (10 SP at 1 contact each x 25 days)
x 30%	Have a family member trading in 90 days
75	**Hot Prospects In Service Each Month**

2. Prospecting In Your Existing Sold Customers Database

In 6 hours of down time, at 5 minutes per call, a salesperson could make 72 outgoing calls every day. *But let's don't even go there.*

So being realistic – have each salesperson call just 10 sold customers or anyone else in your VSA® (in JVTN®) or your CRM using those 5 questions.

2,500	Contacts per mo. (10 SP at 10 calls each x 25 days)
x 30%	Have a family member trading in 90 days
750	**Hot Prospects In Your Own Database**

Total (1 & 2) ... <u>825 More Hot Prospects</u> Per Month!

HOW TO REALISTICALLY INCREASE SALES
149 UNITS & EARN 6 x YOUR NET

With 825 hot prospects per month from 10 salespeople
making just 10 calls each and just one service contact per day...

What is the <u>realistic</u> low-side potential in a 100 unit dealership?

825	Hot prospects
x 60%	Appointments (this will be closer to 70-80%)
495	Appointments made
x 60%	Will show (this will be closer to 70-80%)
297	Appointments show
x 50%	Will buy (this will be closer to 60-70%)
149	Deliveries
x$2,500	Average gross per unit
$372,500	**Additional gross per month from prospecting**
x 12	Months
$4,470,000	**Additional 'Good Gross' each year**

The Sky's The Limit With Prospecting

Your Annual Net Profit Improvement

x 60%   Good Gross to Net Profit

$2,682,000 Additional Net Per Year

Your potential improvement in prospecting is higher than the
total improvement from the floor traffic you have now, and you
could never buy enough extra leads to hit an extra $2.6 Million.

Just imagine your potential
if you did everything we've covered.

(Your cost: $1,270)

With $2.6 million realistically at stake from prospecting, remind me again why
dealers spend $500,000 a year to run price ads instead of teaching salespeople and
managers how to control your dealership's sales, growth and profit each year?

OUR PROSPECTING POTENTIAL

What's The Potential You See?

1. ✍ List the salespeople who can do a better job of prospecting with a step-by-step process and by improving their selling skills – then write in each person's realistic improvement.

   Yep, it's still all about having a clear process, the "selling skills" (asking the right questions in the right order, at the right time), and daily management of their prospecting activities to bring in more of their own prospects with 40% higher gross profit and zero selling expense into the dealership.

Salesperson	Improvement	Salesperson	Improvement
_____	by + ___units	_____	by + ___units
_____	by + ___units	_____	by + ___units
_____	by + ___units	_____	by + ___units
_____	by + ___units	_____	by + ___units
_____	by + ___units	_____	by + ___units
_____	by + ___units	_____	by + ___units
_____	by + ___units	_____	by + ___units
_____	by + ___units	_____	by + ___units

   Total improvement from all your salespeople...   + _____ Units

2. ✍ **The Math:** If our salespeople had clear processes, developed more effective selling skills and prospected each day, I think...

   a. We could realistically sell   _____ **more units per mo.**

   b. Using our total sales and F&I gross of $ _____ per unit

   c. 'a' x 'b' would add *good gross* of $ _____,_____ per month

   d. At 60% of 'c' to net, we'd *net an extra* $ _____,_____ per month

   e. In one year, that extra net profit would be $ ____ , _____ , _____

3. ✍ **WIIFM** (What's In It For Me?) If we did a better job of prospecting every day and delivered those extra units every month...

   I'd personally earn an extra $ _____ per month,

   and that means I'd make $ _____ more per year.

PROSPECTING GOALS
My Action Page & 90 Day Goal

1. Prospecting to find the next buyer in a family is easy. Just ask the right 5 questions at the right time and you'll find the next buyer in the family, almost every time. And 30% of the time, you'll find a hot prospect who'll be buying within 90 days.

    Process: Ask 5 Easy Questions In The Right Order

              • 3 Open Ended Questions

              • 2 'Either / Or' Questions

    Skills: Know The Correct Questions To Ask
    Know How To Respond To Their Answer

    Management: Manage Salespeople's Prospecting Activities Daily

2. ✍ My 90 day goal: We will improve our deliveries from daily prospecting in service, with previous customers, and from our own database of 'Orphan Owners' (salesperson is no longer with our dealership) from ___ or ___ per month now, to a minimum of ____ per month by ___ / ___ / ___.

3. ✍ The steps we'll take to reach our goal on prospecting are...

    1. My goal and plan for prospecting in service _____
        _____
        _____
        _____

    2. My goal and plan for each salesperson to prospect to their own previous customers _____
        _____
        _____
        _____

    3. My goal and plan for prospecting to our 'Orphan Owners' _____
        _____
        _____
        _____

        ✓ Tip: Give each manager a small group of salespeople to train, coach and manage to help each salesperson achieve their individual goals.

4. Focus on prospecting *every day* until you reach your goals. Hold a short management meeting each morning *just* on your goals and progress.

✍ Write Out Your Additional Thoughts On Prospecting
To Reduce Your Dependence On Advertising

_____

_____

_____

_____

_____

_____

_____

_____

_____

_____

_____

_____

_____

_____

_____

_____

_____

_____

_____

_____

_____

_____

_____

_____

_____

Are you seeing the benefits of becoming...

Management Driven vs. Market Dependent

like 80% of your competitors are?

"I feel like I'm getting my degree in sales."

"I have been training on JVTN® for one year and love it. There's nothing better to keep you focused and on track every day!

After attending your Sales Workshop, too, it pulled everything I'd learned on JVTN® together.

After class, I focused on **staying off price, slowing** the sale **down** and **building** the **value** by **asking** the right **questions.**

I normally average 11.5 per month and after class, I sold 19 in April, and 16 in May! Thanks Joe, with JVTN® and your classes, I feel like I'm getting **my degree in sales!"**

– Taylor Robbins, Salesperson
North Country Auto, Presque Isle, Maine

"I was locked in a room with Joe's training for 2 weeks."

"I came to the car business with 25 years of marketing & advertising experience, looking for a change – and came in with an open mind.

I got hired with 5 other people and my manager essentially locked us in a room for 2 weeks with Joe's training. Of the 5 people hired, I was the only one to approach it with **an open mind** and I started absorbing everything and looking for ways to apply it immediately.

In my first month (December), I missed salesman of the month by a half deal and was in first place 5 of the next 6 months, missing the other by just a single ProPack sale. By August, I was the fastest in our 32 year history to be promoted to GSM after only 8 months.

Since I took over as GSM, **our net profits have increased 38% and our employee retention has stabilized.** *Now I spend as much time as possible sharing what JV training can do for people's lives and their careers.*

Thank you, Joe, you made a believer out of me."

– Brian Smith, General Sales Manager
Whiteside of St. Clairsville, Ohio

- and then -

Here's what one of his salespeople told us...

"Joe, before getting into the car business, I worked for 17 years making $17,000 a year. Thanks to the vision and dedication of my manager Brian Smith, and your training on JVTN®, my life has been forever changed.

My first month, I sold 21 units and made $13,000. In my next 3 months, I averaged 20 units and took home over $12,000 per month. My best month so far, I sold 23 units and made $15,000.

In just my first couple of months selling cars,
I made more than in my previous 2 years combined.

I come to **work to work**, I follow all of your **steps to the sale, I never talk price**, and my **customers love me**.

Joe, thanks for the secret to my success and a clear plan I can recognize, duplicate and master for continued future success!"

– Jolynn Peshek, Salesperson
Whiteside of St. Clairsville, Ohio

Let's Talk About Your

Total Potential

In These Top 7 Highest Revenue Sources

Why don't most people ✍ fill in the blanks
and do the math as they're reading this book?
Because 'maybe it's true and then again, maybe it isn't...'

A Dealer in class <u>who did fill in all of the blanks</u>
really hit the nail on the head on why most people don't.

He said that when I say something or toss out a stat or number, *maybe it's true* and then again, *maybe it isn't,* at least for his store.

He said that possibility alone makes it real easy for anyone to ignore what we've covered and justify doing nothing differently tomorrow than they did yesterday.

Then he said <u>*when he fills in the blanks*</u>, the potential from that improvement becomes *true for him, his managers and his dealership.* And once it's *true for him*, it's impossible to say he wants to grow, and then not make the changes *he can and needs to make* to improve.

I agree with him 100%, and I also know a lot of people assume that if they just *think* about how much they could improve, that's enough.

Unfortunately, that assumption is why 97% of the people don't hit their goals. *You have to <u>write out</u> your goals and your plans* to make goal setting work for you. It's the same with potential, *you have to write out your potential* to internalize the impact these changes will have.

So if you haven't already,
go back and fill in the blanks.

By doing that, you'll get a clear picture of what you feel is your real potential, and how to reach it. Plus I guarantee you'll have lots to talk about in your next management meeting.

And if you're unsure it's worth it, go home and say, "Honey, I found out today that I could earn twice as much as I'm making now, do it easier, and in less time so we could have more, do more and so that I could spend more time with you – what do you think, should I do it?"

Seriously now! Just follow the steps on the next few pages
and discover the true potential <u>you</u> see in your own dealership.

YOUR DEALERSHIP'S POTENTIAL

USING YOUR NUMBERS

It's All About The Money

We tossed around a lot of stats and general numbers to see what's going on now in the average dealership and to show you what a great opportunity you have to improve in each of the solutions we covered.

Now it's all about <u>your</u> numbers and <u>your</u> opportunities.

It's your turn to put a number and dollar figure on the opportunities *you believe you found* in these 7 sources to improve your units, your good gross and the net profit in your dealership.

Fill in the blanks in your book, and then go online and use our calculators for some quick "what if" answers on these 7 revenue sources.

Take 2 minutes to fill them out, I guarantee you'll be surprised at how quickly a little potential adds up.

Go to JoeVerde.com/net7

SUMMARY OF YOUR POTENTIAL

✍ What's the potential you see in each solution?
Just copy your answers from each section.

> ### The Potential You See Just From
> **The FLOOR TRAFFIC You Have Now**

1. **How much potential did you find by increasing the # Of Demos your salespeople give to customers already on your lot now? Page 62.**

   a. Unit Improvement Per Month   _____ units per mo.

   b. Good Gross Profit Per Month $ _____, _____, _____ mo.

   c. **Net Improvement Per Year** $ _____, _____, _____ **yr.**

2. **What was your potential to sell more to the floor traffic you have now by improving your salespeople's Core Selling Skills & Processes? Page 72.**

   a. Unit Improvement Per Month   _____ units per mo.

   b. Good Gross Profit Per Month $ _____, _____, _____ mo.

   c. **Net Improvement Per Year** $ _____, _____, _____ **yr.**

3. **How much potential did you find in Gross Per Unit by training your salespeople to focus on more value & less on price? Page 90.**

   a. Unit Improvement Per Month   __N/A__ units per mo.

   b. Good Gross Profit Per Month $ _____, _____, _____ mo.

   c. **Net Improvement Per Year** $ _____, _____, _____ **yr.**

4. **What did you decide it's worth to train managers who work deals and to implement more effective Desking & Negotiation Processes? Page 107.**

   a. Unit Improvement Per Month   _____ units per mo.

   b. Good Gross Profit Per Month $ _____, _____, _____ mo.

   c. **Net Improvement Per Year** $ _____, _____, _____ **yr.**

SUMMARY OF YOUR POTENTIAL

✍ What's the potential you see in each solution?
Just copy your answers from each section.

> The Potential You See Just From
> **UNSOLD FOLLOW UP**

5. How much potential did you find by improving your <u>Unsold Follow Up</u> with the customers who didn't buy on their initial visit? Page 119.

   a. Unit Improvement Per Month   _____ units per mo.

   b. Good Gross Profit Per Month $ ____, _____, _____ mo.

   c. Net Improvement Per Year $ ____, _____, _____ **yr.**

> The Potential You See Just From
> **INCOMING CALLS & LEADS**

6. What was your potential on <u>Incoming Sales Calls & Internet Leads</u> from improving your salespeople's skills and your processes? Page 129.

   a. Unit Improvement Per Month   _____ units per mo.

   b. Good Gross Profit Per Month $ ____, _____, _____ mo.

   c. Net Improvement Per Year $ ____, _____, _____ **yr.**

> The Potential You See Just From
> **DAILY PROSPECTING**

7. What was your potential from training and implementing a <u>Daily Process For Prospecting</u> in service & from your database? Page 139.

   a. Unit Improvement Per Month   _____ units per mo.

   b. Good Gross Profit Per Month $ ____, _____, _____ mo.

   c. Net Improvement Per Year $ ____, _____, _____ **yr.**

YOUR BIG MATH

> ### WHAT'S YOUR
> ### TOTAL IMPROVEMENT
> ### POTENTIAL

A. Your <u>Unit</u> Potential (1a through 7a)

We'd Deliver An Additional _____ Units Per Mo.

We'd Deliver An Additional _____ Units Per Yr.

B. Your <u>Good Gross</u> Profit Potential (1b through 7b)

We'd Generate $ ____, _____, _____ In Addl. Good Gross Per Mo.

We'd Generate $ ____, _____, _____ In Addl. Good Gross Per Yr.

C. Your <u>Net Profit</u> Potential (1c through 7c)

We'd Generate $ ____, _____, _____ In Addl. Net Profit Per Mo.

We'd Generate $ ____, _____, _____ In Addl. Net Profit Per Yr.

D. WIIFM: From the increases above in units and net profit...

I'd personally earn an extra $ _____ per month,

and that means I'd make $ _____ more per year.

'Potential' has never been the issue.
*Now that you understand what you can do,
the most important question is 'will you'?*

Summary...

Now, let's look at what the potential net profit is in that hundred unit dealership, if you improve in these 7 areas.

The Realistic Net Profit Improvement
We Just Covered In A 100 Unit Dealership

$6,671,988

I understand that's too much for most. So take away prospecting,
and you'll still have the potential to improve the net profit by...

↓

$3,989,988

Still a little too strong? OK, then take away any improvement on
phones and internet leads, and you can still improve the net profit by...

↓

$3,611,988

Still kinda high, huh? So also take away any improvement
on unsold follow up and the net will still go up by...

↓

$2,405,988

Really! Still too high? Whatever – just skip the
improvement on desking and you can still up the net by...

↓

$2,286,000

Too high? You're joking, right! OK – assume your salespeople
can't possibly stay off price to build value, you'll still have an extra...

↓

$1,800,000

Are you saying they can't even learn to sell?
I'm not buying it, but that still leaves an extra...

↓

$900,000

**Additional net profit by doing nothing
but improving your number of demos.**

Your Top 7 Highest Revenue Sources

Will you get all the improvements we outlined? Probably not, but when you're looking at $5 Million to $10 Million a year in potential net profit in a 100 unit dealership, let's not kid each other – you can double your net just by improving in these 7 highest revenue sources – and with just the opportunities you have now.

When you focus on these good gross sources, you'll find you never go back to asking those, "What's the budget," questions to try to drive more traffic, or saying, "Let's give up some gross this weekend so we can sell more units."

Instead of focusing on ads or compromises to sell more, start asking more 'what can we improve' questions in these 7 highest sales and revenue sources.

Ask yourself...

- What's our percentage of write ups to traffic? How about deliveries to write ups? Who can improve, so we can improve sales & good gross?

- What's our demo ratio? Who needs to do more demos? What's the plan?

- How are our managers doing working deals – are we sticking to 'budget focused negotiations' or have we slipped back into 'price focused'?

- What about gross – are we giving our customers the chance to pay more by building value? Who has the lowest gross, so we can improve it?

- What about prospecting in service and on the phone – how are we doing with that? Which salespeople can improve? Which manager can help?

- What's our status on incoming calls and internet leads – how are we doing converting those into appointments that show? Where can we improve?

- Are we getting contact info on our unsold prospects? What percent are we getting back on the lot for another chance to make the sale?

Now instead of just hoping the ad will work, you have 7 easy solutions you can implement any time to increase your units, gross and net profit.

Continually find your 'low point' in these skills, processes
and activities and then set your goals to improve.

How will you know which area to focus on?

Start tracking everything in sales using the VSA® in JVTN®. When you do, the information you'll gather will point right to the solution you need to focus on, to increase sales and profits.

Why use our tracking instead of the tracking in your DMS or CRM? Because if you use our training, we'll talk the same language, and your DMS and CRM don't focus on these areas or track the same way we do.

Become 'Management Driven' Not 'Market Dependent'

The real foundation for continuous growth is becoming management driven instead of being an advertising / price / market dependent dealership. When you do the things we've covered, you become 'management driven' by default, and that means you'll never have to worry about having a great economy or perfect weather to deliver more units and turn a profit.

"What's the catch to pulling this off?"

Well the 'catch' is all of those thoughts you've had as you were reading this. Thoughts like, "I don't see how can I pull this off because..."

- I know I can count on (<u>name</u>) to jump in 110%, but will I get past (<u>name</u>)'s resistance? He's the manager who'll fight any change we try to make.

- I don't see how I can do this now, until we get a better team in place.

- We're shorthanded – I don't see how I can train and make sure salespeople are doing what they should, and still do everything else I have to do.

- How will I handle (<u>name</u>)? He's our worst nightmare in the sales department and turns everybody's heads, but he's got protection from the top down.

There's so much more I need to cover, but I just can't squeeze it all in here. So if you do see the potential to improve – do these 3 things right now...

1. Get the Dealer and GM and as many other managers as possible to attend our Dealer / Manager 'Team Leadership' Workshop on how to hire, train, set goals, manage, motivate, and lead your salespeople to more success.

   If this book opened your eyes *some* on the potential you have, when you leave that workshop you'll be floored that there are so many things you can do to control your sales and profits.

2. Get my 'Recovery & Growth' book for the dealer and every manager and *read it* with your managers. Every 'catch' above and more you'll run into on getting everyone to do their part in the plan to grow is covered. If you hate reading, just make sure you read chapters 13 and 30, 31, 32, & 33. The information in those 5 chapters is critical to your growth. (It's free.)

3. If you aren't on JVTN®, sign up now and make one commitment – *follow our directions on the 4 courses to cover first.* When you do, you'll see more enthusiasm, confidence and results than you ever imagined, and you'll understand why some dealers have been on JVTN® since 2005, when we introduced it.

If you've hung in there and read this far, I know you've started to see the real potential in yourself, your salespeople and in your dealership.

Congratulations! Enjoy your success, call us with any questions, and please let us know about your results.

*Your growth is only limited
by your ability to see more potential.*

*Think possibilities, set goals, and develop
the skills you need to get you there.*

– Joe

Results

---

*From averaging 8 per month to 12, and improving their
front end gross from $760 to $1,300 – in 90 days with JVTN®.*

"When I got in the car business 6 years ago, my manager had me watch Joe Verde over and over for the first week. I came out of the gates hungry and ready to apply what I learned. By my second month I was top salesperson, that continued for 3 more months and then I was promoted to finance manager. Recently I took over training our new salespeople – we have daily meetings with JVTN® and they also train on their own. In July, they were averaging 8 units/month with $760 front end gross, and now 90 days later, they are up to 12 units and grosses are up to $1,300! Joe Verde's training gave me my start in the business and I know I wouldn't be this successful without it, so thank you Joe!"

*– Andy Beam, Finance Director
Brookfield Chrysler Dodge Jeep Ram, Benton Harbor, Michigan*

From 118 to 150 cars a month – with 6 salespeople!

"Joe – I wanted to share some success with you that we've had after being avid JVTN® users and attending your Manager's Workshop.

Last year, we averaged 118 cars per month. In March, I went to Train The Trainer and I sent my finance director to the Manager's Workshop and we sold 150 cars with our 6 salespeople.

I want to give credit to your trainers and a lot of help from our JVTN® rep. She calls and monitors all of us on a daily basis and does a tremendous job at it and got us back on track.

Thanks Joe!!!"

*– Scott Braga, General Manager
Boch New To You Superstore, Norwood, Massachusetts*

Results

From 57 to 184 units a month!

"About a year ago while on vacation I brought Joe's book, 'A Dealer's Guide to Recovery and Growth'. We have since attended Joe's 2-Day Manager Workshop and implemented JVTN®.

Our dealership has completely turned around, we now have a sales process that everyone follows, we track everything we do, set goals religiously, and have weekly training meetings with our salespeople.

We were selling around 50 units a month, and in March we had an all-time record month and sold 184!

Joe, thank you for getting us on track and pointing out that there is no secret to success, it's working smarter, not harder like we were doing."

– Marvin Potter, General Manager
Matthews Auto Group, Vestal, New York

I improved my skills and had my biggest month ever with JVTN®!

"I have been in the car business 16.5 years and I've been training on JVTN® for 5 months. When I say training on JVTN®, I mean watching the training chapters, taking great notes, taking the tests and practicing getting the words just right by saying the scripts out loud repeatedly. I learned the importance of bypassing price on the lot, not skipping any steps and to always be asking for the sale.

I sold 15 units in May, 15.5 units in June and 13 in July. By the way, it was my biggest month in pay ever in July! I took home $12,500, which was over $900 per car and I took 8 days off for a vacation! Joe, thanks for an incredible easy-to-follow process that when applied as you instruct…just plain works!"

– Dan Nouguier, Salesperson
Toyota of Northwest Arkansas, Rogers, Arkansas

Results

I doubled my gross and doubled my income with JVTN®.

"I went from never having sold a car to finishing my year at 132 deliveries. I've doubled my gross and doubled my income, making more money than I could imagine. My customers love me because I provide a car buying experience that is both fun and easy, and I love going to work to work every day, I love my job, and I love my dealership! Thank you for the best year of my life!

Joe as you always say – your success in the car business is based on YOU: your selling skills, work habits, attitude and your choice of customers (SHAC). If it wasn't for JVTN®, your trainers, and your incredible support staff, I wouldn't have made it. Your training has made it possible to achieve so many of my dreams: a new car, new truck, a new SUV, a motorcycle."

– Monte Riddle, Salesperson
Primasing Motors, Lebanon, Oregon

My first year selling cars – I sold 157 vehicles and earned $80,000 with JVTN® and your 2-Day Sales Workshop!

"Joe, I just wanted to thank you for helping me sell 157 vehicles and earning $80,000 my first year in the car business.

I've been training on JVTN® and I attended your 2-Day Sales Workshop, which has given me the skills to be a professional in sales.

My first full year, I had the best CSI in the dealership. I had a 70% return with an average score of 95% that was unheard of. My next step is to earn $100K like your book says. I'm just a few steps away, all thanks to you."

– William Stanfield, Salesperson
Pathway Hyundai, Ottawa, Ontario

Results

"My units and gross improved 60%!"

> – Craig Runshe, Sales Manager
> Hubbard GM Center, Monticello, Indiana

"We doubled sales at our dealership in less than 4 months using JVTN®!"

> – Leigh Ann Sumrall, New Car Manager
> Atwood Chevrolet, Vicksburg, Mississippi

"From 10 to 16 after JVTN® and your class..."

> – Bruce Dubrow, Salesperson
> Fred Beans Chrysler Jeep Dodge, Doylestown, Pennsylvania

"Your training has been the best money we ever spent!"

> – Randy Point, Vice President
> Menholt Auto Group, Billings, Montana

"33% increase in units with JVTN®..."

> – Tammy Roach, General Manager
> Brown's Volkswagen, Charlottetown, Prince Edward Island

"From 14 units to 25 after JVTN®..."

> – Prentiss Farsee, Salesperson
> Andrew Toyota Milwaukee, Wisconsin

"I went from green pea to dealer with your training..."

> – Joey Prevost, Dealer
> MacCarthy Motors Terrace, Ltd., Terrace, British Columbia

EDUCATE SALESPEOPLE DAILY WITH JVTN® ONLINE VIRTUAL TRAINING AND INCREASE YOUR NET PROFIT

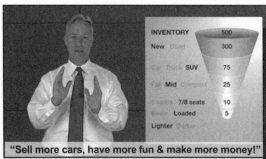

"Sell more cars, have more fun & make more money!"

"Train on JVTN® & get 50% more write ups!"

You know *what* to do to double your net profit.
Now teach your salespeople *how* to do it.

Figuring out how to increase unit sales and net profit is easy, and actually doing everything we've covered isn't that difficult either.

You will have to train your salespeople, because no matter how hard you try, or how much you spend to put more traffic on the lot, and no matter how badly you wish or believe they should step up, figure it out, and take action on their own – they just can't do things they don't know how to do.

Start making more sales right away.
Just try training *correctly* with us for one year.

Make a commitment to training with us the right way for just one year and you'll never consider going back to the huge ad budgets, lost sales & profit and constant turnover with average and below average salespeople.

You don't need to spend *extra* money on training, just take it from your ad budget. Don't worry, training isn't that expensive and you'll have plenty of money left over for *targeted ads* and even more sales.

Read through the comments and incredible 'overnight' results in this book that salespeople and dealerships are getting with JVTN® and call us!

Training is the least expensive, highest ROI you can buy.

Don't Miss Another Sale – Call Now (877) 417-6211

10 MILLION REASONS WHY
YOU SHOULD TRAIN ON JVTN®

Should you do what others are doing? Yes, but only if it's working and they're actually getting results. JVTN® covers both. Over 10,000,000 chapters of our online courses have been taken by salespeople and managers who get immediate results by developing the critical skills we cover that 90% of the salespeople would never learn otherwise.

Follow my directions in setting up and using JVTN® as your daily training source, and you'll be shocked at the differences from day one.

Selling more and increasing your gross profit will be immediate, and you'll win hands-down against the competition, year after year.

SELLING MORE REQUIRES BETTER SKILLS & PROCESSES

We aren't the razzle-dazzle guys and we don't do sound-bites in our workshops or online.

We clearly explain critical processes you need like: selling, closing, negotiating, follow up, handling calls & leads, and a dozen+ others. Then we teach and help your salespeople and managers develop the skills it takes to master each specific process.

ACCOUNTABILITY ... TESTING • REPORTING • CERTIFICATION

Every course we teach online includes workbooks for everyone, quizzes on every chapter, a complete leader's guide for every manager to follow, and a final course certification test that can only be taken with a passing grade for the course.

JVTN® will give you 'live' reports on every chapter (in progress %, pass / fail) by salesperson, team, or by dealership for dealer groups, and you can access these reports anytime, from any location.

"I've made sure JVTN® has your back in every critical area to guarantee your success with our training. Start today and see results tomorrow."

Start Training Now (877) 417-6211

JOE VERDE MANAGEMENT & SALES TOOLS

Make Record Sales – Get Joe's 2 Monthly Newsletters

• **Selling Cars Today –** Salespeople need new and updated information every day. Use Joe's easy to read, monthly newsletters for your daily training. Each month, they're filled with winning sales strategies guaranteed to keep your salespeople on track and moving toward the winner's circle every day.

• **For Sales Managers Only –** The only monthly newsletter written just for Sales Managers. With new information to help you hire, manage and train your sales team for success in today's new market.

Newsletters are available both online or in print.

Books For Salespeople
Get copies for everyone today!

• **Manage Your Career In Sales: Goal Setting for Salespeople**

Are you ready to get what you want in sales? If you're serious about taking your career to the next level, Joe's book will show you how to totally control your sales and income every month and every year.
Get your printed copy (shipping rates apply) or get your free PDF download today!

• **Earn Over $100,000 Selling Cars – Every Year**
Your potential selling cars is incredible. You can get lucky and make $10,000 in one month. But you won't get lucky enough to make over $100,000 every year – that takes skills and a plan.
Get your printed copy (shipping rates apply) or download your free PDF today!

• **How To Sell A Car Today**
Close almost 50% of the people you talk to if you follow the "Steps To Selling" in this book 100% of the time, with all of your prospects. Let's take your sales, income and career to your next level.

• **38 Hot Tips**
Here's an easy way to increase your sales right now! Inside are 38 great ideas on how to sell more cars in today's market and answers to common sales questions.

Plan For Your Success

• *Plan Your Day, Plan Your Week!*
Weekly Pocket Guides

The hidden problem is daily activity management. Make it easy with this on the lot pocket-size weekly planner for your salespeople.

• *Plan Your Month!*
Monthly Planning Guides

For Sales: Set goals, measure your performance, create your plan & increase your income!

For Managers: The easy way to track, forecast, set goals and follow up with your sales team.

--- **For Dealers Only** ---

A Dealer's Guide To
Recovery & Growth

Get the book that will change your life with a common sense, step-by-step process you can follow to grow your dealership. If you're struggling, follow these steps and be profitable in 30 days. If you're making money, follow these steps to double or triple your net profit. Available for print and free download at JoeVerde.com.

Don't Miss Another Sale – Call Now (877) 417-6211

✍ My 'To Do' List

_____

_____

_____

_____

_____

_____

_____

_____

_____

_____

_____

_____

_____

_____

_____

_____

_____

_____

_____

_____

_____

"If you think you can do a thing or
think you can't do a thing, you're right."
– Henry Ford

✐ My 'To Do' List

_____
_____
_____
_____
_____
_____
_____
_____
_____
_____
_____
_____
_____
_____
_____
_____
_____
_____
_____
_____
_____
_____
_____
_____

"If you think you can do a thing or
think you can't do a thing, you're right."
– Henry Ford